Make
EVERY
PENNY
Count

Make
EVERY
PENNY
Count

Budgeting tips and tricks to keep more money in your pocket

Ricky and Naomi Willis

Creators of the Skint Dad blog

PIATKUS

PIATKUS

First published in Great Britain in 2024 by Piatkus

3 5 7 9 10 8 6 4 2

A CIP catalogue record for this book
is available from the British Library.

ISBN 978-034943-942-6

Typeset in New Baskerville by M Rules
Printed and bound in Great Britain by
Clays Ltd, Elcograf S.p.A.

Papers used by Piatkus are from well-managed forests
and other responsible sources.

Piatkus
An imprint of
Little, Brown Book Group
Carmelite House
50 Victoria Embankment
London EC4Y 0DZ

An Hachette UK Company
www.hachette.co.uk

For Beth, Daniella and Chloe –
everything we do is for you x

Contents

Part Two: Make Money

Part Three: Manage Money

Introduction

Hello and welcome to our book!

If you're reading this it means you've taken the first step towards not being skint any more – that's amazing! You won't look back, we promise.

At Skint Dad we are all about helping everyday people make every penny count. We're a husband-and-wife team, Ricky and Naomi Willis, who have been running Skint Dad together since 2014. But we're not financial experts with degrees in accounting, and we're not in the business of investments or crypto or stocks and shares. But we are really proud that over the past few years, we've made Skint Dad one of the biggest and most popular destinations for financial guidance in the UK and grown a loyal following of people who are fed up with being skint – just like we were – and want to do something about it.

Our message is simple: being skint sucks, but you don't have to sit in a room with the light bulbs unscrewed and only eat pasta for ever if you want to get out of debt and save for your future. Yes, you will have to make some sacrifices and change the way you do things a bit, and we're here to show you how and what to do along the way. But it is possible to live well and enjoy your life without the worry of debt hanging over you, or coasting along with nothing put away for a rainy day. You don't have to sell everything you own or work three jobs (unless they're side hustles: we'll tell you about those!) you just have to work smarter and make every single penny count. We all waste so much, whether it's our time, money, food or energy. Whatever you're doing, there's probably something else you could be doing to make all your assets and skills work harder for you. Our family is living proof that you can make your money go further, you just need to learn how to make every penny count. And the good news is, we're here to guide you through.

So how did we end up here, telling you how to manage your money? When we got together in 2008, we had two children between us (one each from a previous relationship) and pretty soon there was another on the way! We both had full-time jobs, but like a lot of people, we could never seem to make ends meet. Childcare costs for our youngest were way more expensive than when we'd had our older kids, and for Ricky, commuting to London meant travel costs were huge as well. We found ourselves taking out more and more credit cards and payday loans just to get by. At one point we realised we owed money to twenty-five different credit companies – catalogues and store cards, credit cards and loan companies. This was just to cover our rent and supermarket bills and keep the girls in nappies and school shoes. We weren't living a lavish lifestyle or going on expensive holidays, we just couldn't afford life.

But the crazy thing was, we didn't ever talk about money. Like a lot of people, we grew up believing money was something private, something you should be discreet about. So we just kept kind of muddling through, paying off bills here and debts there, without ever stopping and really looking at the whole picture. We did try to make a budget occasionally, but we were never able to stick to it. (We know now that we were doing it all wrong and we'll show you how to write a budget you can and will stick to.)

Eventually, we worked out that it would actually save us money if Ricky gave up his job – at a printers in London – and stayed at home to look after our youngest daughter, who was still a baby at the time. The cost of rail travel to London and childcare was simply outstripping what he earned and it made no sense to keep losing money the way we were. He asked for a pay rise but there was no spare money in the pot at work. Naomi's job was closer to home and she could walk there, and so it was the only choice.

Even at that point, people on the outside – including our closest family and friends – didn't realise what was happening for us financially. Sure, we had no childcare costs, no travel costs – but now we only had one wage. So even though we weren't spending much, we were still borrowing more and more. Ricky felt awful that Naomi was the one financing our life, but we both felt so ashamed, as though we had failed at the very basics of being parents.

Around the same time, the blogosphere and parenting sites like Mumsnet had bloomed and there were lots of mums starting their own blogs online. Ricky enjoyed talking to people on Twitter (now known as X) and came up with the idea of starting a 'dad blog', really just to stay sane. He'd tried a few baby groups but he was always the only dad there and felt quite isolated as a stay-at-home parent. As we had money worries, the name Skint Dad seemed to fit, and he started writing in August 2013. His first articles were about the general business of being a stay-at-home dad: looking after Chloe, what was happening in *Peppa Pig* and who was going to win *The X Factor*.

Then one day, we realised we had £6.20 in the bank and there was still a week to go until payday. We'd maxed out on all our credit cards, reached all our overdraft limits and scoured down the back of the sofa for every last penny – there was nowhere else to find any money. We'd been broke before, but this time we really began to panic. We had a baby and children at school, how were we going to feed them? Ricky said he wanted to write about this predicament on the blog and share what we were going through, but Naomi didn't want the world to know about our problems. We had a big argument that evening and when Naomi went to bed, Ricky stayed up late writing his blog.

Here's what he wrote:

It's the 17 September, still a week away from payday, and all you have left is £6.20 to your name. In the cupboard there is only enough food to feed your family for three days and on top of this your one-year-old only has four nappies left.

This is the situation we found ourselves in this month. We knew it would be tight financially, it always is, but this month was worse than others. Normally, a week before payday we at least have enough food to last even if there isn't any money left.

For the first time in a long time, we had gotten ourselves into a situation that I was unsure how to get out of. We'd always struggled financially but never to this extent.

The good news (if you can call it that) is we did make it through to payday, we did survive.

SURVIVING ON THE BREADLINE

First of all, we needed to set some priorities. There was us, our nine-year-old daughter Daniella and our one-year-old daughter Chloe living at home. Beth, our eldest, was living at her mum's but Ricky still paid child maintenace for her as well. We needed to eat and Chloe needed nappies.

These are what we wrote down on a scrap of paper in order of importance:

1. Feeding the children
2. Nappies for youngest
3. Feeding mum and dad

Next, we went to the kitchen and made a list of all the food we had in the cupboards, fridge and freezer. It wasn't a great deal but more than we presumed. We worked out that with the food we had in the house, if we were careful, we could feed the children breakfast, lunch and dinner for four days.

This would mean me and Skint Mum missing out on 'proper' dinner a couple of times but we were OK with that.

So that left us with three days' worth of food and nappies to purchase. It was getting late and we were both emotionally shattered so we went to bed. I didn't sleep much that night. It was 2 a.m. when I last looked at the time. Lots of things were going through my mind.

I felt like I'd let my family down by getting into this situation. I kept having flashbacks about bills coming through the door, creditors ringing demanding money, and me having to borrow from anywhere and anyone just to keep our heads afloat. I had let them down.

The next morning Naomi left for work and Daniella left for school, leaving me and Chloe to go to the shops and try to make our £6.20 stretch as far as possible. The first item I looked at was nappies. We normally bought Pampers but I obviously couldn't afford them so I grabbed the cheapest ones I could find. It was the shop's own brand, twenty nappies for £1.41. I was concerned about the quality but what else could I do?

Next on to the food. I had just under a fiver left so I headed straight for the pasta which I knew would be reasonably cheap. Grabbing three bags of basic shapes for 29p per 500g I started to think we could do this. Pasta sauce next, two jars cost 39p per 440g and I could split the jars if I had to. I then headed to the frozen aisle where I picked up twenty frozen sausages for 91p and a 1kg bag of frozen mixed veg for 75p.

That left me £1.48 which I used to buy two tins of new potatoes for 15p each, two tins of beans for 25p each and six bananas. When I arrived home I put the kettle on, sat Chloe in the lounge, laid all the food we had and what I had bought on the kitchen side. We had done it. We had enough food to last until more money came in the following week.

OK, I'll admit, the food we had wasn't the most nutritious, also there wasn't really any variety, but at least we could eat. At least when I put my children to bed every night I knew they had full bellies.

Today is payday and it all starts again. After all the bills are paid we don't have much left. The last week has really opened my eyes to how close we actually are to the breadline every single month. I've realised we cannot carry on living paycheck to paycheck because it's not living, is it? It's surviving.

Starting from this month, Skint Mum and I are going to make some changes. We are going to stop surviving and start believing. Believing that we don't have to live like this. Believing that we can make a better life for our family. I don't want to live in poverty. I don't want my children to grow up thinking this is normal. We want a better life and I'm going to use everything I have to achieve it.

That blog post changed everything for us. The next morning, we woke up to literally hundreds of messages from people all over the world, sharing their own money worries and giving us their advice and tips. The post was shared and re-shared on social media everywhere and we even had journalists from national newspapers calling to talk to us about it. It was really a very humbling experience to hear from so many people and it was so reassuring to realise others were in the same boat – we were not alone. It felt like we had taken the first step to dealing with being skint.

When the blog post was shared on the front page of Mumsnet and we started to read all the comments by parents who were also worrying about how to feed their kids, things began to fall into place. It made us realise that we had something important to say, something that we could really work with, and it was a way to hold us accountable for getting our finances sorted. We decided to share our entire budget online, for everyone to see, and people were really interested. So we continued to tell our story, talking about money and how we were getting ourselves out of debt. As more and more people signed up for our newsletter and read our blog posts, the Skint Dad community was born.

Four years and a lot of blog posts and research later, we realised our dream and were both able to go full time running Skint Dad. We've never been about having flashy cars or designer clothes; we've never wanted the kind of ostentatious wealth some people might chase. We just want to have a nice home, go on holiday with our girls, eat out from time to time, and be able to sleep at night without worrying about debts and living month to month. We've finally achieved that financial freedom and now we're sharing everything we've learned with you. And, while we're still Skint Dad by name, the advice we're sharing here is as meaningful and helpful for non-parents and single people, young and old, as it is about those of you who are raising families.

We're not going to bamboozle you with financial terminology or complex maths – that's not what we're about. We simply believe in making every single penny count, whether it's your monthly wages or 5p you found in an old coat pocket. It's all about thinking smarter so that you can do things you love and enjoy this precious life. You'll find what we share is always simple, honest, and no-frills. But most importantly it's achievable. Because if we can do it, so can you!

We've broken the book down into really easy to follow sections. In Before We Start, we show you how to create a budget that you can genuinely work with, share why budgeting doesn't need to be dull and how it can be your best friend on this journey. Then we've broken money down into three key sections: Save Money, Make Money and Manage Money. We've learned that getting back on track isn't only about reducing spending, getting a better paid job or finding a savings account that works for you, it's a combination of all of these things and loads more. So, within each section, you'll find loads of ideas, tips and advice, plus personal stories from us and members of the Skint Dad community to inspire and motivate you. We've also included contact details for all of the organisations that can help you on your way, so you've got everything you need for making every penny count, right here at your fingertips.

Sound good? Ready to get started? Let's go!

Naomi and Ricky x

Before We Start

LET'S TALK ABOUT BUDGETING

It wasn't until Naomi and I sat down and really talked with each other about our finances that we began to make any kind of real progress. It was something we knew we needed to do, but when your finances are out of control, budgeting can feel like an overwhelming task. Either that or it just seems a bit boring. We used to think that too! But by taking control we've grown to actually enjoy the budgeting process – it helps us see the whole picture and gives us choices. With the knowledge our budget gives us, we decide where our money goes, instead of our money telling us what we can and can't do. Budgeting means financial freedom, and there's nothing boring about that. You just have to do the groundwork.

So put all your preconceptions to one side, stay with

us, trust the process, and see what making a budget can do for you.

READ THIS BIT FIRST ↓

Our tips for getting the most out of your budget

1. Find a way that works for you. We love an Excel spreadsheet, but not everyone is the same. There are some great budgeting apps out there these days that can help, or maybe you prefer an old-fashioned pen and paper. It doesn't matter how you do it, what matters is that you feel comfortable working with your budget and – most importantly – you can easily use it and update it. Think of your budget as a living thing that needs regular attention, not a lot of rules set in stone.

2. Be honest with yourself. There's no right or wrong and no one is coming to tell you off about your budget! Being really honest with yourself is the ONLY way to do this. So if you have a secret scratch card habit or know you probably spend more than you can afford on clothes each month, put it all in there. Only by looking at it all in one place will you get a clear picture and be able to start making changes. Online banking can

be really useful in helping you see where your money is going and what you are spending it on.

3. Be realistic about what you can and can't live without. Becoming debt free and having a bit put aside definitely means making some sacrifices, but at the same time, there's no point pretending you can simply cut something significant out of your life overnight, as you'll only end up back at square one.

4. Don't worry if you don't know all the exact amounts to begin with, just try to make realistic estimates and always round up your totals. Rounding up, even by just a few pence, gives you a little buffer to help when something unexpected happens or when certain things fluctuate in price; for example, it's a busy month for birthday presents or the price of your supermarket essentials have gone up.

5. Talk about it. Whether it's a partner, a friend or an online community, sharing your decision to get serious about your finances is a great way to make yourself accountable. Checking-in with other people also helps you realise what you're going through isn't anything to be ashamed of. We should all talk more about money; it is only discriminatory employers and credit lenders who thrive on our silence.

Self-employed? Or get paid weekly? Sometimes it can feel like the world is only set up for people who earn a monthly income. We know how confusing it can be to have to think about what you spend on something every month, when you don't always get paid every month. Again, there are some great apps out there now aimed at helping freelancers and sole traders manage their money. But if you want to keep things simple, the best way to get a good estimate of your monthly earnings is an equation where you divide your last annual income total by 12.

Say your income last year was £24,000

Divide it by 12

Your monthly income is going to be £2,000

Now, some months you might not earn £2,000 and others you might earn more. But if you have that number in your mind as the maximum you will bring home in a month, you will at least be able to make sure your outgoings don't exceed what you can afford. It's not pinpoint accuracy but it's good enough to get started with! Remember your budget is a living thing, so you can come back to it and tweak it as much or as little as you need to.

Being self-employed can be great for things like flexibility and job satisfaction, but it takes real focus and commitment to manage your finances. You can do it. Start with a budget.

CREATING YOUR BUDGET

Now you've committed to creating your budget and shared your exciting news with others, it's time to write everything down.

This is how we do it:

1. Split your budget into categories.

    The first category should be your Income. Write down everything you have coming in, no matter how small:

    -   Wages
    -   Benefits/Tax Credits
    -   Maintenance (if you are a single parent)
    -   Side hustle

The next category or categories should be all your Fixed Expenses. These can include:

- Mortgage/rent
- Household bills
- Council tax
- Debts (credit cards, loans)
- Transport (car, train, etc.)
- Sinking fund
- Savings

You can have as many categories as you like. Some people like to see every single cost; others are happier to group costs into general headings such as 'Energy bills'. Do what works for you – just be honest with yourself about what's going out.

Fixed expenses should not include variable costs like your food shop or petrol, or nice-to-haves like clothes or make-up.

That sinking feeling

A lot can change from month to month and unexpected costs can creep in from anywhere. It might be an issue with your car, a school trip or even a leaving meal with colleagues at work. There are also things you know will likely happen each year at some point, but can't be sure when, whether it's a car service, school uniform or a new pair of glasses. While you can't always accurately predict which costs are going to come in when, you can put a small amount aside throughout the year so that you're ready for them. This is your sinking fund. It's slightly different to a regular savings account in that you can and probably will need to access it, and it's for specific costs such as the ones mentioned above.

It's generally not a good idea to try to save when you have debts – because debt usually costs you more in interest than anything you can earn on savings – but a sinking fund is always a good idea, whether you have debts or not.

You can keep your sinking fund in a savings account or if you have a bank account that allows you to create pots or pockets you can keep your sinking fund in one of them. But be very clear about what the sinking fund is for and try not to dip into it for everyday costs like food shopping. It's there for when you're sinking!

Your third category should be your Variable Expenses. This includes food, clothes, entertainment and general day-to-day living such as:

- Supermarket shop
- Clothes
- Netflix/other subscriptions
- Football season ticket
- Personal care (hairdressers, cosmetics)
- Kids' clubs/school trips

These costs are likely to change and fluctuate every month, which is why it's so important to have a budget planner you can easily access and update.

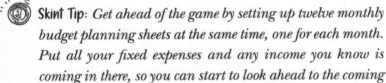 **Skint Tip:** *Get ahead of the game by setting up twelve monthly budget planning sheets at the same time, one for each month. Put all your fixed expenses and any income you know is coming in there, so you can start to look ahead to the coming months as well as manage your current month's money. This can be particularly useful if you know you are going away or will be spending more money in a particular month.*

2. Now you have your Income and your Fixed and Variable Expenses, you can work out what you have left for the month by simply taking your Expenses away from your Income.

If you are lucky enough to have money left over, there's plenty you can do to help it grow. We'll show you how in the next chapter!

If you don't have any money left over or find you are spending more than you are earning, this is the moment where everything changes. We'll help you turn things around, keep reading!

This is what a typical monthly budget looks like in our house:

Monthly Budget July 2023	
Income	
Pay (after tax)	£2,500.00
Side hustle	£100.00
Benefits	
Pension	
Other income	
Total	£2,600.00
Outgoings	
Household bills	
Mortgage/rent	£700.00
Council tax	£100.00
Gas	£50.00
Electric	£50.00
Water	£30.00
TV licence	£15.00
Home phone/broadband	£40.00
Mobile	£40.00
Digital TV	
Car insurance	£20.00
Home insurance	
Other insurance	£30.00
Debts	
Loan	£70.00
Credit card	£50.00
Hire purchase	
Other	

Misc expenses	
Car maintenance	£ 30.00
School trips	
Vet bills	
Other	
Living costs	
Food	£450.00
Fuel	£60.00
Transport	
Road tax	£10.00
Child care costs	£40.00
Kids clubs	£40.00
Subscription	£10.00
Entertainment	£50.00
Clothing	£50.00
Personal care	£10.00
Other	£10.00
Savings	
Emergency fund	£150.00
Savings	£150.00
Children	£50.00
Christmas/birthdays	£50.00
Opticians	£10.00
Total outgoings	£2,395.00
Total income minus total outgoings	£205.00

 Skint Tip: *Now have a go at doing your own budget and see what it looks like. And take a moment to give yourself a pat on the back. If you've come this far you're already well on the way to finally being in control of your money.*

Next up: Learn how to save more of your money, the Skint Dad way.

Part One

SAVE MONEY

I f you're like us you might have grown up thinking that saving money is the same as being tightfisted or penny-pinching or plain old mean. What we've learned – mostly the hard way – is that being an effective money-saver is not about being reluctant to spend your cash; it's about being *smarter* with your cash so you actually have MORE to spend on the stuff you want. Everyone's goals and circumstances are different, but the one common idea that all of us on this money-saving journey can share is that saving money is ultimately about trying to achieve the standard of living we want, and doing it in the most economical way possible.

In this section, we're going to look at some of the ways you can start to spend smarter and save your money on life's essentials. We'll show you how changing your mindset from broke to frugal can help you kickstart your saving journey, and we'll explore the different ways you can save cash on everyday stuff like your supermarket shop, eating out and household bills. And, if you're parents like us, we've also got some ideas for saving money on all the kids' costs, and helping them learn to save along the way as well.

Let's get started.

1

BECOMING FRUGAL

We want you to forget any negative associations you might have around being frugal and begin to see it for what it is – common sense. Your time is precious, your energy is precious. Your earnings and income represent your time and energy, so why would you want to spend your hard-earned money on things you don't need or want? Frugality is just plain logic. It's the practice of applying a considered, informed approach to where and how you spend your money in order to maximise its value.

But when you've been raised on a diet of easy credit and pay-later deals, being frugal can be a bit like learning a foreign language. It takes time and practice. It's also something that means something different to everyone. We can't tell you how to live your life; what's important to you might not be important to someone else. And that's OK. For frugal living to work, you've got to do it your way.

The good news is it's easy to start behaving like a saver right now, wherever you are. You don't need to open a new bank account or skip meals to start saving money. You can make small, simple changes at home and in daily life that will lay the foundations for a more prosperous lifestyle and leave you with a few extra pounds in the bank, without really trying.

Here are some tips for making the switch to frugal living that will help you on your way.

1. **Create a budget.** Hopefully you read the previous chapter so you've started making a budget already. But we put it here again just in case you haven't done it yet. Nothing is more important in your money-saving journey than this, so if you haven't done it yet, start doing your budget now!

2. **Learn to shop around.** It can be so tempting to just throw things in your trolley or hit 'Add to Basket' without checking to see if you can get it cheaper elsewhere. But the difference in price for the same item in different stores can be staggering. Just a small change in your behaviour can help you save £££s so try to remember to shop around, especially on large items or on things you buy regularly.

Skint Tip: *Supermarket and shopping comparison websites are really useful for this and do the hard work for you. Check prices on your favourite products before you shop.*

3. **Switch lenders.** It doesn't sound very exciting but spending some time switching bank accounts, credit cards or loans can save you significant amounts of money. Switching your credit card debt to a zero-interest account is a no-brainer, just don't forget to switch again before your zero-interest period ends! (There's lots more on credit cards and loans on page 168.)

4. **Grow your own veg.** This doesn't have to mean digging up your whole garden and turning it into a smallholding (although if you can do this, it will save you even more). Just planting some lettuce in window boxes or growing some tomatoes from a hanging basket will give you fresh salad all summer, save you money and bring you quite a lot of satisfaction, too.

5. **Bake your own bread.** Use your loaf (ahem) and get into baking your own bread. A decent bread-maker is a real investment and over time you can make countless loaves from store-cupboard ingredients. Plus you'll come to prefer the fresh taste and goodness of your own bread over shop-bought. Now who's the breadwinner?

Skint Tip: *You don't need to buy the latest, most expensive breadmaker. Check your local Facebook Marketplace for second-hand ones and cut your costs even more. Some bread recipes don't even require a breadmaker, so try a few different recipes before you buy one.*

6. **Make do and mend your clothes.** Instead of throwing away a pair of jeans because they've got a hole in them, give them a quick repair and extend their life. It's so simple but so many of us still get rid of clothes that have got loads of life in them. Dyeing your jeans and other items is also a great way to keep them alive for a while. Give it a go and put the money you've saved in your mended pocket instead.

7. **Wait before you buy something.** Sometimes it can seem like the world will end if you don't have the thing you are about to buy immediately. But it won't, and you can wait. And often, when you decide to wait, the need for it disappears. Next time you are coveting something, see if you can wait a while and notice what happens when you do. You might be surprised to find that you forget all about it!

Scarcity impulse

Ever heard of the scarcity impulse? As humans we are predisposed to want and keep things that are scarce more than things that are in abundance; it's part of our caveman programming from when things like food really were scarce and we had to hoard it to survive. Today we don't have to worry so much about finding an antelope to kill for tea and keeping the leftovers in our cave, but retailers are still really good at tuning in to our deepest impulses. Things like Black Friday and Prime Day, or even smaller 'While Stocks Last' or 'Sale' promotions can have us feeling like we need to buy something quickly before it runs out. We're not saying they're all a con – sale prices can be very helpful! – but it is worth being aware of how retailers push stuff at us so that we buy it. Next time you feel you have to buy something because it's on sale and might run out, ask yourself if it really will run out and if you really do need it. Chances are you'll realise it's your scarcity impulse kicking in.

8. **Borrow your baggage.** Or anything that you only use once or twice a year, especially travel items like luggage, camping equipment, wetsuits.

Unless you are off somewhere every weekend, you probably don't need to own this stuff and have it sitting around your house for the rest of the year. Ask friends and family if you can borrow these items, and enjoy handing them back when you've used them!

9. **Share your skills.** Babysitting circles, lift shares, sewing skills, odd jobs – whatever you can do, you can offer it in return for something you can't! Lots of communities have swap-shops for items and services. If you haven't got one near by, why not set one up?

10. **Switch off when you leave.** It's amazing how many people still leave the lights on when they leave a room. Get into the habit of switching off every time you move to a new room. It will save you pennies in the moment, pounds in the long run.

11. **Ditch the tumble dryer.** Yes they're convenient but fresh air is free and better for the environment. Plus your clothes last longer when they're not regularly tumble-dried. In the winter, when drying outdoors is harder, a heated drying rack is a far more energy-efficient alternative.

 Skint Tip: *Put fewer clothes in your wash and put them on a spin cycle – they'll be less damp when you get them out and take less time to dry. You'll thank us for this one!*

12. **Go veggie.** Meat is expensive. You don't have to give it up entirely, but try to designate at least a couple of days a week as vegetarian. You'll see a big reduction in your shopping bills.

13. **Get smart about appliances.** It uses more energy to boil a kettle when it's full. Turn off anything that you might usually leave on standby. Turn the fridge off if you're on holiday (but make sure there's nothing in the freezer!). Don't leave chargers 'on' when they're not charging a phone. All these things cost you money, why waste it?

14. **Get smart about your household products.** There are so many alternatives to the big brands that you see on the supermarket shelves. You can make your own laundry detergent really easily, use reusable laundry sheets or try an Ecoegg. In the bathroom, try lemon and vinegar instead of spray cleaner. Some supermarkets offer compostable carrier bags that can be repurposed for food waste – or poo bags if you have a dog. Shampoo bars are an affordable, waste-free alternative to expensive bottles. See which 'essential' products aren't so essential after all.

DIY laundry detergent

It's so easy to make your own laundry liquid. Next time you finish a bottle of branded product, try making your own and pour it in to the old bottle. The ingredients can all be picked up at the supermarket and you can keep the leftover ingredients for the next batch. No more crazy expensive laundry liquid in your weekly shop!

You'll need:

- 200g soda crystals
- 50g bicarbonate of soda
- 120 ml liquid soap (plain, unscented)
- 2 litres of boiling water

To make:

In a bowl, add 500 ml of boiling water to the soda crystals and stir until dissolved. Gradually add the bicarbonate of soda and keep stirring until it's also dissolved. Then add the liquid soap and the rest of the water, stir well and leave to cool. Once cool, whisk it up until it is smooth and pour into your bottle. Use as you would your regular laundry liquid.

15. **Ditch the takeaway coffee.** If you're someone who buys a cappuccino every day, take a minute to work out what that is costing you per month and think of what you could spend it on instead! Making your own coffee at home can be a lovely ritual. Whether you're a French presser or an instant kind of person, find the way that works for you and enjoy your morning brew in the knowledge that you are saving money.

Do the coffee maths. Say you buy a coffee on the way to work every day. It's only £3, but do you realise how much it is costing you per year?

£3 cappuccino x 5 = £15 a week
£15 x 4 = £60 a month
£60 x 12 = £720 per year

ON COFFEE!

16. **Plan your meals.** This one simple process will transform your shopping habits and cut down drastically on waste.

The Skint Dad guide to meal planning

Meal planning isn't complicated. It just takes the randomness out of your supermarket shopping and helps you avoid coming home with things you won't eat. You just write a list of the meals you'll have for breakfast, lunch and dinner each day in the coming week (we plan for seven days but you can plan for more or less if you prefer), and then you just shop for those items (told you it wasn't complicated).

If you struggle to find inspiration or know what to cook you can look online for meal planning templates and suggested weekly shops. You don't always have to stick to these lists; it's just a great way to take the stress out of cooking every day and wondering what to have for tea.

If you've got kids, it's something they can get involved in and helps to build healthy spending habits. The key to success with meal planning is to stick to what your list says and don't throw a bunch of extras in at the last minute. It takes a while to get used to shopping like this but once you make it a habit it can be really enjoyable to get out of there knowing you haven't given in to the temptation of those delicious-smelling doughnuts in aisle 3!

17. **Make friends with your freezer.** Dashing out to buy something for dinner is rarely cost-effective. Having something home-made in the freezer takes a lot of stress out of mealtimes and helps your shopping go further. Also, supermarkets often reduce the price of food that is about to reach its sell-by date. Buying this and freezing it can shave £s off your shop.

18. **Make your own gifts.** The most meaningful and unique gifts are things people can't buy themselves. Try making jam, cordial or pickles and put them in recycled jars. Scrubs and creams are also really easy to make and look great in recycled bottles. Reuse old wrapping paper to cover the lids or to make your own labels. You have a really unique and special gift, all for free.

19. **Exercise for free.** There is no need to spend fortunes on gym memberships or fitness classes. All movement is exercise so get out for a walk or run or do a free online workout at home. If you can leave your car at home and ride a bike or walk to work, even better. If you find you need motivation from others, buddy up with friends and create your own fitness group. There are loads of apps that can help you stay motivated, and accountable.

20. **Use public transport.** Save on petrol and all the other costs of owning a car by using public

transport as much as you can. You can read or listen to music on your commute, and it's better for the environment, too. No-brainer, this one.

21. **Do an energy audit.** Insulation, solar panels and double glazing can all make a huge difference to the amount of energy you use. If you rent, ask your landlord to make sure they have done everything they can to help you keep your bills down. And be sure to check with your local authority for grants that might be available.

22. **Eat seasonally.** The food that's in season is always the cheapest. It also happens to be exactly what you need nutritionally for the time of year. If your veg has been flown in from Kenya, it's probably lost all of its goodness on the way anyway.

What's in season?

Winter: parsnips, potatoes, beetroot, pumpkin, sweet potato, Brussels sprouts, cabbage, carrots, cauliflower, apples, pears, quince

Spring: asparagus, cucumbers, spinach, spring greens, gooseberries, rhubarb

Summer: green beans, lettuce, runner beans, courgettes, squash, tomatoes, blueberries, strawberries, raspberries, plums, currants

Autumn: mushrooms, rocket, sweetcorn, potatoes, pumpkin, squash, pears, plums, elderberries, damsons, sloes

23. **Dispose of disposables.** Whether it's switching tampons for a Mooncup, single-use razors for refillables or paper napkins for cloth ones at the dinner table, replacing disposables with reusable items is an easy switch that's good for the planet and good for your wallet.

24. **Learn some frugal recipes.** Lots of the big-name chefs have got budget-friendly recipe books out and there are plenty of websites devoted to cooking on a shoestring. Teach yourself a few budget recipes so you know them down pat; that way it's never a chore to knock up something cheap and cheerful whenever you need to.

25. **Buy second-hand tech.** We have an unhealthy appetite for new stuff, especially when it comes to tech. Used and refurbished phones and laptops are, more often than not, just as good as their factory-fresh counterparts. Most electronics

firms also offer a like-new refurbishing service, so it's always worth checking what you can get refurbished before you buy the latest upgrade, There's usually very little difference and you can get a fantastic new item for a fraction of the price.

26. **Make your own compost.** If you've got a garden or outside space it's super-easy to make your own compost and help your garden grow for free. Many local authorities provide free compost bins and information about how to make your own, plus they'll deliver them for you! Water butts are also a great way to save rainwater for use in the garden and can often be bought at discounted prices from your local authority – check with yours and see.

27. **Buy second-hand clothes.** We've already mentioned fixing or upcycling your clothes to make them last longer, but sometimes you need to buy new clothes. Whether it's for growing kids, a special occasion or you need a refresh, you can still get clothes without breaking your budget. Skip the shop sales and look to buy second-hand. There are a range of places you can try, such as charity shops (not just in store as some have eBay shops too), apps like Vinted or Depop, or why not try a clothes-swapping event. If you don't have one near you, consider starting one with friends.

28. **Get cashback on all your shopping.** Some people think being frugal means not spending any money. However, we believe it's about spending money more wisely and with a considered approach. So, when it comes to having to part with your cash, we always make sure to make money back. This can easily be done when shopping online with cashback websites such as Quidco or TopCashback. The sites are free to join, and it won't cost you any more to shop through them. Find what you want to buy, then click through and checkout like usual. The cashback site tracks what you spent and pays you back a percentage or set amount. This adds up to hundreds of pounds back in tax-free money over a year! Cashback can be made on everything from groceries to clothing, tech, toys, holidays and insurances.

29. **Take advantage of best-before food bargains.** Buying discounted food can be an eco-friendly and wallet-friendly way to keep your food costs down. Supermarkets often mark down items nearing their 'use by' or 'best before' date with yellow stickers, making them cheaper – we've seen food dropped to as low as 10p! Shopping during late afternoons or evenings can increase your chances of finding these deals. Another option is the Too Good to Go app, which partners with retailers, cafés and restaurants to offer

surplus food at reduced prices. Through the app, you can reserve a Magic Bag filled with surprise items. Always check expiry dates and make use of your freezer, taking into account what you have in your week's meal plan. There are online shops such as Approved Food and stores on the high street that sell surplus and short-dated food mega cheap. Check locally if you have a food waste or community café in your area. These cafés offer meals for a bargain price using food from super-markets that would otherwise be wasted.

Case Study

Shirley is married and as well as her husband, has two hungry teenage sons to feed. She reduces the cost of her supermarket shop by buying up lots of yellow sticker items in the supermarket. She picks up bargains on foods including fruit and veg, meats, cheese, treats, and ready meals. If they can't be used that day, she freezes them for another day. Nothing is wasted. Shirley regularly shares the meals she makes for the family in the Reduce Your Supermarket Spend Facebook community group, and reckons on a good day she can save around 85 per cent on the shelf label price!

30. **Ditch your subscription TV.** Cutting your TV
    subscription can be a savvy way to save money.
    And you needn't sit with nothing to watch in
    the evening as there are loads of other options,
    so you can still watch your favourite TV shows
    and films. For basic watching, Freeview gives
    you access to numerous TV channels at zero
    cost. Newer TVs generally have channels built
    in, or you can buy a cheap box to pick up the
    channels and even record them. You can also
    use on-demand streaming services. The main
    TV channels offer a free service for catching up
    on recent TV as well as access to vast libraries
    of other content. There are also paid streaming
    services, such as Netflix, Amazon Prime and
    Disney+, and if you pick one or two it will still
    work out cheaper than subscription TV. YouTube
    may be full of funny cat videos, but there are
    also many documentaries and programmes to
    watch for free. Your local library is also always
    worth checking out as many offer DVD rentals
    at minimal cost.

2

SAVING FOR SKINT PARENTS

Nothing will ever prepare you for the joy of having children – or the cost! As parents, we know only too well how expensive raising a family can be. Whether you're a traditional 2.4 kind of tribe, a single parent or a blended family, there is no getting around the fact that children and family life are expensive.

However, there are plenty of things you can do to protect yourself from the shock of new expenses and to keep costs down, no matter how old your children are. We've done the hard work for you, so here's everything you need to know about saving money when you've got kids.

PREGNANCY

Once the news has sunk in, you'll no doubt want to start planning for your new arrival. Which cot is best? What kind of buggy or car seat will you choose? There are hundreds of brands out there all vying for your business, and it's really easy to spend a lot of money on things you think you'll need. We know how exciting it can be to plan for a new baby, but try to stay calm and wait before you go out and buy everything under the sun. Babies really do need very little and it is worth sitting tight to see what you need once the baby has arrived. Of course, there are some essentials you're going to have to have and the good news is that you have got plenty of time to get yourself sorted.

Freebies

Nearly all local authorities and the major mother-and-baby brands offer some kind of free gifts or starter packs for mums-to-be. Whether it is nappies, books or, if you're in Scotland, a baby box that acts as a first cot, there's lots of good stuff out there that you can have for free! Spend a morning searching online and sending off for as many of the packs and kits as you are entitled to.

Parental leave and pay

If you are employed you will be entitled to parental leave. What you get paid during your maternity is your *maternity pay*. Maternity pay is usually a combination of Statutory Maternity pay (from the government) and Company Maternity pay, which is often dependent on your length of service. Partners are also entitled to one to two weeks of paid paternity leave; again this is dependent on service so be sure to ask.

Talking it through with your employer, an HR contact or even colleagues familiar with the process should help you understand things better. Some employers pay you a full salary during your maternity leave; others pay less the longer it lasts. Every employer and contract is different. Talk to your employer as soon as you can to be clear about when you'll take maternity leave and what your pay will be.

If you are going to be taking a long time off work and earning significantly less over a long period, you can start to build a buffer for the shortfall now by putting extra money into your sinking fund or a separate savings pot. If you have a partner, now is also a good time to think about taking shared parental leave and how you will divide the time between you. Paid parental leave is not exclusive to women. Adopting parents are also entitled to maternity pay, so make sure you check out what you can get – from your employer and from the government.

Self-employed or a sub-contractor?

If you don't have an employer, or if you haven't worked for your employer for long enough to qualify for maternity pay, you can still receive statutory maternity pay from the government. It's unlikely to match your pay, so it's worth getting savings in place ahead of the game. Start building a maternity leave fund as soon as you can!

 Skint Tip: *If you receive certain benefits you may be eligible for a Maternity Grant. Check out what's available to you on the gov.uk website or ask at your local Citizens Advice.*

Find your village

They say it takes a village to raise a child. Having a support network around you, whether it is family or friends, will help you be the best parent you can be for your baby. Having a grandparent or uncle or aunt around who is willing to help with the baby when you go back to work will also save you money on childcare. Start to have these conversations as early as possible so that you can work out what your costs will be.

Baby showers and stocking up

These are a great opportunity to stock up on the things you'll need before your baby arrives. Don't be afraid to let people know which items you would welcome as gifts; it makes no sense for anyone to give you things you don't need. Ask for clothes in a range of sizes (not only newborn) so that you have clothing for your baby to wear for months to come.

If you're not having a baby shower it's still a good idea to stock up on some of the essentials that you know you're going to need to buy repeatedly once your baby arrives. We're talking nappies (again, not only in newborn size), wipes, baby-grows, nappy cream, and all those products that babies need so much in the early months. Keep an eye out for promotions and discounts while you're expecting and you can save loads of money – and time.

NEW BABY

Your baby is here! Chances are you won't have much time to think about anything other than feeding, sleeping and changing nappies for a while. But the time goes by so quickly and soon you'll be getting out and about with your new arrival. Having a new baby needn't be expensive, it's a time of simple pleasures, but there are still plenty of things you can do to keep costs down during this lovely stage.

Check your benefits

All children in the UK qualify for Child Benefit and this should be paid to you as soon as your baby is born. If you receive certain benefits you might be eligible for others once you have children, so it is always worth checking. The charity Turn2us is a great place to get free, confidential advice on your entitlements.

Nearly new sales

So much baby stuff gets used so briefly! You can find great second-hand and nearly new items at local sales, often arranged by the NCT or other local charities and groups. Facebook Marketplace, Gumtree and eBay are all great for finding bigger items like cots and buggies.

Toy libraries

Instead of buying new toys, try using a local toy library. Like a regular library but for toys, they enable you to find something new and interesting for your baby to play with. Plus you don't get bored of looking at the same bits of plastic lying around the house! Best of all, it saves you a fortune on buying new toys.

Make your own baby food

There are so many great guides and recipes online to help you with weaning when the time comes. Apart from the obvious benefit that you get to be sure you are feeding your baby all the right foods, making your own also means you aren't spending money on shop-bought baby food. Invest in some good storage pots and you can take your own baby food when you're out and about as well. Freezing your home-made food also means you've always got something for them when hunger strikes.

Open a Junior ISA or Premium Bonds

It is never too early to start a savings account for your baby. Junior ISAs earn better rates of interest than those for over-16s, so it's worth opening one as soon as you can. Interest rates go up and down, but the fact remains that if you can save £100 a month from the time your child is born, at an average of 5 per cent interest, you will save around £35,000 by the time they turn eighteen. Quite the numbers, eh? It's the kind of figure that could fund a university degree or put a decent deposit on a house. So it makes sense to start saving for them sooner rather than later.

For more on ISAs and other ways to save for the grown-ups, head to page 165.

Skint Tip: *We get it, £100 a month is a lot of extra cash to find! You don't have to save that much, but if you want to hit maximum final figures, you could start saving before they are born to allow for lower contributions. Or, ask grandparents and family to chip in and watch your child's nest egg grow.*

 Skint Tip 2: *Watch out for fees and commission costs on some ISAs, which can gradually eat into your children's savings over time if they are not effectively minimised and managed. You can accomplish better results if you save in accounts that are free from income and capital gains tax.*

Use washable nappies

Washables have come such a long way in recent years and today's options are far from the clumpy, complicated things they used to be. Washables are also a great way to save some cash. If you consider your child could be in nappies for a few years, it's definitely worth it in the long run.

Some local authorities now offer vouchers, free kit, nappy libraries and even cashback, to encourage new parents to use washables. Others offer kerbside laundry collections and will collect and wash your nappy liners free of charge. This is because of the huge volume of waste caused by disposable nappies. Unfortunately, the schemes vary across the country, but check with your local authority and see what help you can get. The Nappy

Alliance can also help with information and guidance on what's best for your budget.

NURSERY AND PRE-SCHOOL

Before you know it your little one will be off to nursery or pre-school. How many days and hours they do each week will depend on you – everyone's situation is different and you'll find the way that works for you. Children in the UK are all entitled to an amount of free childcare provision in a pre-school or nursery setting, but it differs in each country so make sure you find out what you can get. You might also want to start thinking about a childminder or nanny, or get relatives to help with pick-ups and drop-offs. If you're a working parent, this is where the juggle really begins!

HELP

If you're going back to work you might find that you need help with picking up your child from nursery or dropping them there in the mornings. You can get help paying for this as long as it is 'approved childcare'. This means nannies, childminders and staff from nurseries and playgroups. The person needs to be Ofsted registered – you can't get help to pay your parents or partner, unfortunately! The waiting lists for good approved childcare providers are usually very long so it's worth getting ahead of the game on this one.

 Skint Tip: *Fancy being a childminder? If you want to stay at home with your child for longer and enjoy looking after other children, you could become a childminder. You don't need any qualifications or prior experience to set yourself up as a childminder, but you'll go through a registration process that covers first aid and ensures the care you give is safe and that your home complies with regulations. There are also grants available to get yourself started. It's a great way to get free childcare and earn at the same time.*

Packed lunches

Welcome to the packed lunch years! If your child is going to nursery or pre-school they'll usually need a packed lunch. Lunches don't need to be expensive, and are the cheapest way to ensure your child gets a healthy meal. But there is nothing more disheartening than opening a lunchbox at the end of the day to find a lot of food uneaten and gone to waste. It is therefore a good idea to really think about what goes in their lunchbox and make sure it's something they will eat. This is also a good opportunity to get your child thinking about money and shopping early on. Get them involved in planning for their lunches and talk about how much things cost and the idea of waste and why it's bad.

Skint Tip: *There are a lot of lunchbox-sized snacks and foods out there that are often just regular food cut up into small sizes for small hands. It's great to give your child bite-size foods, but you can avoid the extra cost and the pointless packaging of 'lunchables' and just chop things up yourself! Keep some small pots and tubs in your cupboards for lunches.*

Some of our family favourites for healthy pre-school packed lunches that are great for small hands:

- *Cheese chunks and mini crackers*
- *Carrot sticks and hummus*
- *Pitta bread slices with marmite or peanut butter*
- *Mini sandwiches with ham or cream cheese*
- *Chopped up apple, grapes or cherry tomatoes*
- *Slice of home-made cake or plain biscuits*
- *Hard-boiled egg*
- *Chicken breast chunks*
- *Cold pasta*

SCHOOL YEARS

Uniforms

According to figures from the Children's Society, the average cost of a new school uniform is over £300. That's a lot of money to find, especially in the summer holidays. A new Education Act in 2021 made it compulsory for all state schools to make their uniforms more affordable and so you can now pick up generic items for school uniforms and PE kits in supermarkets and cheap high-street retailers.

But even if they're cheaper, there's still a lot of stuff to buy! From bags and pencil cases to blazers and shoes, it really is a big expense for any family. The good news is that there are plenty of ways to cut the costs.

- Buy second-hand at school sales and/or local online pages.
- Ask friends and family for any hand-me-downs.
- Buy in stages. Children rarely need all their kit on the first day of term so ask the school what they need and wait until you buy anything else.
- Check you really need it. Sometimes uniform lists are old and haven't been updated, so find out if your child definitely needs their initials embroidered on their games top before you get it done!

Skint Tip: *If you receive certain benefits you might be able to apply for a school uniform grant. It's a bit of a postcode lottery, so check with your local authority to see if yours can help.*

Skint Tip 2: *Depending on your occupation or the industry you work in, you may also be eligible for a free grant to help pay for school uniforms. Check on the Turn2us site for information on what funds and grants may be available.*

School lunches

Lots of children love school dinners and with our busy lives it can be reassuring to know they are getting a hot meal at school. However, if you are paying for school lunches five days a week the costs can really add up. Some ideas for keeping the school lunch budget down:

- Mix it up and do packed lunch for four days and school dinners on Fridays.
- See if you're eligible for free school meals (the money goes onto your child's school payment account so no one needs to know they're free).
- Get your kids involved in making their own lunches. Owning a decent food flask means they can take their home-made soups, pasta and even reheated leftovers into school.

 Skint Tip: *Hungry teenagers can eat you out of house and home if you're not careful! Make sure all your school lunch foods are kept somewhere 'safe' where teens with the munchies can't devour them at all hours.*

Transport

Obviously, walking is the cheapest and most convenient way to get your child to school. There's no parking hassle, you save on petrol, they get good exercise and it's a lovely time to have a chat with them. Walking is so beneficial that it is worth factoring in some extra time to include the walk to school if you can. Maybe you can do some work calls on the way home or have a run. But if you live too far away from school and your children can't walk there, you might find yourself having to get them there under your own steam. If that's the case:

- Many councils and schools offer transport grants for children; make sure you check out what help is available.
- Trip-chain your morning commute. If one of you is heading to work, can you drop off your child at school on the way? Even if school is not directly on your route, combining the two 'links' in your morning chain might be more cost-effective than having two cars go out each morning. If the timings don't work, can you ask your employer about a different start time or drop your child at school earlier and save on the petrol that way?
- Buddy up with other families and share lifts to and from school.
- Get on your bike! Children benefit from the exercise and fresh air of a bike ride before school, and getting there under their own steam is a great confidence boost for them too. Most schools and councils run schemes that teach kids the basics of cycling so that they can feel safe and competent on

the ride to school. Ask at school or your local council about cycling schemes and, as always, buying second-hand is your friend. Children's bikes don't need to be state-of-the-art, they just need to work and be safe. A regular service will help them stay in good condition for longer, too.

Pocket money

At some point during the school years the subject of pocket money will probably come up. We've talked a lot about pocket money with the Skint Dad community and what we've learned is that there is no one-size-fits-all approach. And that pocket money is a really divisive subject. One thing is clear – no matter what your child says, *all* the other children in the class *don't* get a lot more than they do.

Some parents give pocket money to their children from a very young age, others wait until they're in their teens. Some believe it should be earned, with chores and jobs around the house. This teaches children that money doesn't grow on the proverbial trees and that they can't expect to have their own money unless they work for it. Other parents think it's OK to give pocket money regardless of chores. They argue that children should be helpful around the house anyway and that having a little bit of money in their pocket (or online app!) teaches children how to budget with what they've got and that they can't always do a chore to earn more. Whichever side of the fence you fall on, there's no denying that pocket money is a valuable lesson in the way the world works.

 Skint Tip: *The most important thing, when you are considering what pocket money to give and when, is to make sure you can afford it! It's the old airplane logic of saving yourself first. There's very little point in giving your child money if it means you have to go without. Don't forget: you're the one putting food on the table. As always, go back to your budget. What can you spare? Be realistic and don't make promises to children that you might find tricky to keep.*

This is how we do pocket money in the Skint household.

1. We don't give pocket money for no reason. For us it needs to be associated with a chore. We live in a busy household and apart from the valuable lessons that chore-associated pocket money teaches about earning, we also really need everyone to do their jobs so we can stay on top of the house. Chores might include:

   – Vacuuming and dusting
   – Emptying the dishwasher or doing the dishes
   – Putting the recycling out
   – Looking after younger siblings

2. We encourage our children to split their pocket money. Some can go into a savings jar (piggy bank) for short-term savings. This pays for all their essentials, like sweets or magazines they like to read. The rest goes into their savings account (Skint Dad does an online transfer), and they can keep that money for longer-term savings goals like the trainers they want or a new games console they're hoping for.

3. How they split it is up to them, but we always talk to them about how they're going to split it and what the benefits or disadvantages are of putting some away or keeping some in the savings jar. And we keep a record of it in a little notebook, so they can look and see what has gone where. We also look regularly at their savings account (Junior ISA – more on ISAs on page 165) online so they can understand the concept of interest and see why saving can be a good idea. We've found this gives them a real sense of control and empowers them to turn things down if they would rather put their money away. (When our daughter announced she wanted a ukulele, we said she had to save up for it. She did, and she bought her own ukulele, knowing that it was what she really wanted.)

Neither of us had conversations with our parents about money when we were growing up, so it's really important for us as parents to break the cycle and have open, honest conversations about money with our kids. Why don't you start a money book with yours and see what happens?

 Skint Tip: *Talk to your children about the bills when they come in. It doesn't have to be scary for them, you can ask them what they think about the price of energy or get them to help you add up the costs this month. It's a great way to get them involved in budgeting and in helping them to apply the maths they learn at school in the real world.*

Pocket money apps – good or bad?

If we are heading for a cashless society is there any point in kids having cash?

Pocket money apps really work for some people – there's no losing your money down the back of the sofa and other family members can send money to your child on birthdays and Christmas. Some apps even let you set chores and have savings options too.

We're not against them, but our feeling is that it is still worth teaching kids about money with old-fashioned coins and notes. Why? Think of them as the tools of the trade. Without knowing how to hold a pencil, a child can't write. Without knowing how to hold a pair of scissors a child can't cut paper. Without handling real money and knowing how many pennies make a pound, or being able to visualise a 50p coin as half a pound, children don't get to really understand money, they're just moving numbers around in an app.

If you do decide to use an app for pocket money, you don't need to pay for them. Paying a fee to a bank so you can give your own child pocket money is the ultimate rip-off! And remember that from age eleven, children can have their own bank account with a cashpoint card. Pre-loaded debit cards are also useful if you're concerned about them losing money but don't want to get involved in subscriptions. The message here, as always, is: do your research!

TEENAGERS

Teenagers get a bad press sometimes but it is true, they can be rather challenging! Especially when it comes to money. They are more independent and, if they're older teens, able to go places by themselves, meet up with friends and all the other things that teenagers do. Plus they want clothes and trainers and all the latest make-up. It's an expensive time for parents and emotionally challenging as you grapple with hormones and moods. But the teenage years are also a great opportunity to teach your child about managing their money and instil some healthy habits that they can take with them in life.

1. Get a job! Teenagers can have part-time jobs from the age of thirteen, although before they're sixteen there are restrictions about how many hours they can do. If they're keen to get a little weekend job and start to earn their own money that's great, but make sure they're working for a responsible employer who meets the guidelines around young people and work. All the latest information and regulations are on gov.uk.

2. Phones and technology. Rare is the teenager who doesn't have a phone these days, and it is reassuring to know that you are able to contact them while they are out and about. But phone contracts can be expensive, especially if the whole family needs a phone! Encourage your teenager to work out their own set-up. A pay-as-you-go sim-only deal puts them in charge of their own data and minutes. When it comes to handsets, think second-hand refurbished, or can they have a hand-me-down from a relative? Can they sell an old handset to help pay for their new

one? (More on selling handsets on page 127.) Buying and maintaining their own phone and managing their monthly limits gives teenagers something to be responsible for and conscious about, and is essentially another form of budgeting. Owning and maintaining and paying for a phone is a great metaphor for the world that lies ahead for them, so it's good practice not to hand it all to them on a plate. And if they need more data (teenagers always need more data), there are always jobs they can do to earn it!

3. Learning to drive. For many teenagers, learning to drive is a rite of passage. The promise of independence and the thrill of being behind the wheel are hard to resist. However, getting a driving licence doesn't come cheap. There are lessons, the cost of the test, buying a car, insurance and ongoing maintenance to consider. This is an excellent opportunity for teenagers to learn more about budgeting and saving. They can contribute towards lessons or even the cost of their first car. It gives them a taste of the real world, where large expenses require careful planning and saving over time. Shopping around for car insurance can be an insightful lesson in value-for-money and understanding contracts. Encourage your teen to approach driving with a financial perspective, making them not only

a responsible driver but also a mindful spender. This will set the foundation for future significant financial decisions in their adult life.

BLENDED FAMILIES AND SINGLE-PARENT FAMILIES

Like a lot of families today, we are a blended tribe. We both have children from before we met each other and we also share a daughter. Managing the money around blended families can feel a bit like sewing together a patchwork quilt, with child maintenance and children living between different households and all the other costs that are involved when families split and merge. Every family situation is different, but both parents are by law financially responsible for their children. How you work out who pays for what is down to individual circumstances, and working out finances with an ex or a new partner can often be tricky. That's why it's extra important to make savings where and when you can.

We can't tell you how to work out your finances but if you find it's hard to do by yourself there is plenty of help available for single-parent families and those trying to navigate finances post-divorce.

- **Turn2us** is a charity that helps you find the benefits and grants that are available to you.

- **Gingerbread** is a charity that helps single parents; there is lots of advice on their website about navigating finances as a single parent.
- **Family Lives** is a charity that supports parents and families in all aspects, including coping with post-divorce situations.
- **Child Maintenance Service** is there to help parents work out a financial arrangement when they've separated or if they've never been in a relationship.
- **The Money Advice Service** is funded by the UK government and offers free and impartial money advice, covering topics from budgeting to benefits.

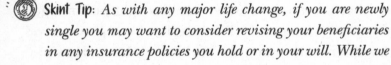 **Skint Tip**: *As with any major life change, if you are newly single you may want to consider revising your beneficiaries in any insurance policies you hold or in your will. While we don't want to come across as morbid, it makes very strong financial sense to make sure you protect your family should the worst happen and you can avoid any legal disputes.*

3

EATING OUT

The Skints love eating out! When you work hard and have a busy family life, there's nothing better than having someone else cook for you and do the dishes. It's also a great way to get out of the house and spend time with each other away from the distractions of daily life. Whether it's a date night for the two of us, a family meal or meeting up with friends, the experience of eating out is about so much more than the food.

We know from experience and talking to the Skint Dad community, that when feeling the pinch, eating out is one of the first costs people tend to cut back on. It's a non-essential expense, after all – you can probably feed your family for a week on what it costs to eat out at some places – and that is hard to justify when you're skint. But even when the pennies are down, we all need a little treat from time to time. We've worked out a few hacks that can help everyone, and mean eating out doesn't always mean splashing out. As with most things financial, you just have to shift your mindset a little bit. Here's how to do it:

1. Be mindful of your lunchtime habits. We're all guilty of grabbing a meal deal or heading to our favourite chicken restaurant with colleagues at lunchtime. But these little lunches and daytime snacks add up over time. Try to be more aware of how often you're buying ready-made food at lunchtime (and breakfast if you have an early start and don't eat at home), and ask yourself if that egg mayo sandwich is something you really need to spend your cash on, or if you would rather put the money towards a nice meal out at the weekend. Simply being more aware of your spending habits around small meals can free up quite a bit of cash for special occasions. As always, making a packed lunch is the best money-saving strategy.

2. Skip the starters. It sounds obvious but if you're heading for a posh dinner and you're worried about the bill, it can really help if you decide before you order that starters and so-called appetisers are off the menu. Just dropping this course (or it could be dessert if you prefer, or both) takes quite a chunk off your bill. You still

get to eat out and enjoy an evening away from the kitchen but you don't break the bank doing so. And if you are worried about being hungry with only a main course, maybe you are eating out at the wrong places! Make the decision in your mind before you sit down, so that you are not tempted by what's on the menu.

 Skint Tip: *If you want to make things feel a bit more special, do the appetisers at home. Put out some nice olives or nuts and a glass of your favourite tipple before you go out. Or buy a nice pud from the supermarket that you can tuck into when you get back.*

3. Bring Your Own booze. There are still plenty of independent restaurants with a BYO policy. As restaurants tend to mark up a bottle of wine by about 300 per cent this is a definite money-saver. Happy days (and nights)!

4. Don't assume certain things come free. Some restaurants put things like bread and nuts on the table without asking. This is all very nice, but before you start nibbling check they are actually free and you won't be charged for them at the end of the night. The same goes for bottled water – a jug of tap water is free.

5. Check the bill. There's no need to feel embarrassed about taking a minute to check the bill at the end

of the night. Whether it's deliberate or an innocent mistake, staff do get the bills wrong sometimes so check and re-check before you pay. You wouldn't buy a new dress in a shop without knowing what you are paying for it, so it's OK to make sure you know what you're buying in a restaurant, too.

6. Get an everyday discount. Discount cards are great if you've got children and need to feed the family during the holidays or on a special occasion. For instance, thousands of independent and chain restaurants, from Burger King to Ask Pizza, are part of the Tastecard scheme. Depending on the offers, you can get two for one on meals, or money off your bill. Tastecards also offer deals at cinemas, hotels and visitor attractions. Alternatively, if you are buying insurance anyway, with Compare the Market, you can get access to Meerkat Meals where you get two for one or 25 per cent off at hundreds of restaurants across the country, plus money off on pizza delivery, without having to scour the internet for a discount code.

Do the Thirty-day No Eating Out Challenge

If you've done our 1p Saving Challenge (see page 97) then you'll know how motivating it can be to give yourself a goal. If you've had a look at your budget and realised you're probably shelling out too much on dining out, then give the Thirty-day No Eating Out Challenge a go.

As the name suggests, this involves not eating out for thirty days. But it's not all depriving yourself of fun and sitting at home watching *Bake Off*! It's also an amazing opportunity to save for something special and to rethink a few things at home at the same time. Here's how you do it:

1. Go over your bank statements and receipts from previous months to get a rough idea of how often you buy food out (this includes takeaways and lunches-on-the-go – anything you haven't made at home). Now add up the total (you may be surprised!) and whatever it is, put at least half of it into a savings pot. The rest is what you can add to your grocery shop to spend on the extra food you'll be eating at home this month.

2. Eating out is all about the occasion and the ceremony. If you can't eat out, try to set the scene for a special occasion at home instead. This doesn't just mean laying the table with unnecessary amounts of cutlery

and napkins (although it can if you want it to). You could try eating in new spaces in the house. Maybe it's as simple as eating in the garden or arranging a blanket and comfy cushions on the floor. If it's a nice evening take your dinner to the park. It doesn't need to be lavish or cost anything (in fact, it shouldn't cost anything!) but it should let you feel like you're doing something different.

3. Master a few super-speedy dishes to have up your sleeve for when time is short. We all know that sometimes you run out of time to cook or feel too tired to think about doing all the prep involved – that's how Deliveroo gets you hooked! Having a few fast and delicious meals that you can conjure up in minutes means you'll always have an option for when that can't-face-cooking feeling kicks in. Batch-cooking and freezing is also a great way to ensure you have a decent meal at hand.

4. Get the family involved. This is such a great thing to do as a family because everyone can contribute and everyone gets something out of it. Get the kids on packed lunch

duties or designing a tracker that can go on the wall. Have family discussions around meal planning and put some special occasion meals in the diary, whether it's a birthday tea, a movie night with friends or a theme night around your favourite cuisine, you can still have things to look forward to even if you are eating at home.

Now you can add to your no-eating-out savings pot every time you do this challenge.

4

THE BILLS

Saving on bills is like finding hidden treasure in your own home. Imagine, every pound you save on electricity or water is a pound you can use for something else you really like! The first step is understanding what bills you have. Most families have to pay for things like electricity, gas, water and the internet.

Now, the magic starts when you begin to check these bills closely. You'll often find you're paying for stuff you don't really need or use, and you can make simple changes with a big difference in your finances each month.

COUNCIL TAX

Council tax is one of those things we all have to pay, but did you know there are smart ways to make it a bit lighter on your wallet? First off, check if you're in the right band. Sometimes houses are put in the wrong band, and you might be paying more than you should. You can challenge it and even get money back!

If you live alone, or with people who don't have to pay council tax, like students or a carer, you can apply for a 25 per cent discount. Also, certain groups, like pensioners or people on low income, can get a council tax reduction. Each council has its own rules, but it's definitely worth looking into.

And don't forget, you can often pay your council tax over twelve months instead of ten, making each payment smaller and easier to handle.

GAS AND ELECTRICITY

Saving on gas and electricity is like giving yourself a pay rise without even having to ask your boss! To start, let's talk about 'switching' to a different supplier. If you shop around and find a cheaper rate, you could save loads. Don't worry, the lights won't go out while you switch. It's really easy.

Next, let's go on a light bulb hunt. Swapping your old light bulbs for energy-efficient LED ones can make a big difference. They last longer and use less electricity. It's a win-win! Do you ever leave your TV or computer on standby? That's like leaving a tap dripping. Over time, it adds up. So, make it a habit to turn off gadgets when you're not using them. And what about the heating? Wearing a jumper inside so you can turn the thermostat down just one degree can save you money. Don't heat rooms you're not using. Close those doors!

To become more energy efficient, you could look to install solar panels. There is an initial cost, and you may spend from £4,000 to £6,000 for an average home installation. There are some government grants available to help pay the costs. The good news is, they could save you up to £270 a year on your electricity bill, according to the Energy Saving Trust. So, in the long run, they could really pay off! (Be sure to check if you are eligible for a grant as it may take you a long time to earn back the outlay if you're not.)

WATER

There isn't an option to change water providers, but you can do practical things around your home to save the pennies going down the sink. A leaky tap might seem small, but if you're on a water meter, every drip will cost you money. And did you know that if you cut just one minute from your shower time, you can save quite a bit over a year? You can also replace your showerhead for a water-efficient one – they use less water, but it doesn't feel any different. Some toilets have a dual-flush button. Use the smaller flush when you can. If yours doesn't have this, you can put a filled water bottle in the tank to use less water each flush. Washing-up is no fun, but filling a bowl instead of letting the tap run can make a difference to your water bill. Also, if you're waiting for the tap to get hot, catch that cold water in a jug. You can use it for plants or boiling pasta later.

BROADBAND

Broadband, the magic that lets us browse the internet and watch our favourite shows, can be a big bill each month. But there are nifty ways to trim it down. First off, do you really need the fastest speed? Check your usage. If you're just sending emails and watching a bit of telly online, you might not need the speediest option. Downgrading can save you pounds! Sometimes getting your broadband, TV and phone from the same company can save you money. Just make sure you're not adding extras you don't need.

Next, haggle like you're at a market. When your contract is about to end, ring up your provider and ask if they can offer you a better deal. Sometimes they'll drop the price just to keep you as a customer. Check out new customer deals on price comparison sites. They do the hard work for you to show what other providers offer. You can then use it as a bartering tool, or switch if you can save more.

HOME PHONE

The home phone can be a big part of your bills – but do you ever use it any more? If you only have it because it came with your broadband, see if you can get a broadband-only deal. This could save you a bit right away!

If you need a home phone, consider when you use it. Some plans offer free calls in the evenings or at weekends. If that's when you mostly chat, switching to one of these plans could make your bill smaller.

MOBILE PHONE

The mobile phone is a must nowadays, especially as you can use it to shop, pay bills, deal with government services and stay connected. Are you in a contract? Are you paying for unlimited data but hardly using it? Or perhaps you've got tons of minutes that you never use? Even mid-plan, you can ask to downgrade your package to match what you really need. At the end of a contract, if your phone is still in good shape, a SIM-only deal can save loads of money and roll for just a month at a time, giving you more flexibility. Alternatively, use pay-as-you-go and only pay for what you use, so there's no shock at the end of the month, which is a good option to switch to at the end of a contract deal.

 Skint Tip: *Use Wi-Fi whenever you can. This will save your mobile data for when you really need it. Connect at home or in places with free Wi-Fi and save your precious data for later.*

TV LICENCE

We might forget about the TV licence, but it's there, and it costs. So how can we save on it? First, let's look at who needs a TV licence. There has been a huge shift in how people watch TV, so you may be paying when you don't need to. If you only watch on-demand services like Netflix or Amazon Prime and you don't watch or record live TV on any channel, guess what? You don't need a TV licence!

You do still need a licence if you're using BBC iPlayer. So let's say you like BBC programmes and you do need a licence. If you're a student and only need a licence during term time, you could get a refund for the months you're not at uni. It's like getting free months of TV! If someone in your household is over seventy-five or is blind, you might be eligible for a reduced fee or even get it for free. Check to see if you qualify.

TV SUBSCRIPTIONS

TV subscriptions can quickly turn into a monthly money drain if you're not careful. But there are clever ways to enjoy your favourite shows and sports without breaking the bank. Firstly, do you really watch all those channels? Most people have favourites and rarely touch the rest. See if there's a cheaper package that covers what you actually watch. You may also find that moving to a streaming service gets you your favourite TV series bundle, then you can watch channels through Freeview or Freesat, and save a lot each month.

 Skint Tip: *Bundles can be a good deal, where you get your TV, broadband and maybe even your phone service all from the same provider. But be careful and make sure you're not adding stuff you don't need just because it's in a bundle.*

TRANSPORT

Getting around can eat up a lot of your money, whether it's fuel for your car or tickets for public transport. Let's talk fuel first. Instead of driving to the first fuel station you see, there are apps and websites that can show you the cheapest petrol and diesel. This is not only handy for local fill-ups, but also great if you are in a new area. Did you know that driving smoothly, without sudden stops and starts, can make your fuel last longer? Also, keeping your tyres pumped up to the right pressure can help save fuel. And if you're someone who likes to fill your whole tank up, you might want to reconsider – driving around with all that extra weight in the tank creates 'drag' and causes you to use more fuel!

If you're a regular on buses or trains, consider getting a season ticket or a travel pass. It might cost more upfront, but it's usually cheaper than buying a ticket daily. Students, seniors and families can also get railcards that offer discounts.

And don't forget cycling or walking for short journeys. It's free, good for you, and you don't have to worry about parking.

There's more about reducing the cost of getting to work on page 106.

5

TRAVEL AND DAYS OUT

You've got some much-needed time booked off work and want to do something – you deserve a break. But at what cost? The idea of saving money on holidays, days out and travelling is often met with scepticism. It's easy to assume that fun experiences are bound to be expensive, but that doesn't have to be the case.

We love to spend time in London visiting museums with the children. The key to keeping the costs down isn't to cut out experiences but to approach them wisely. It's not just about hunting for discounts or pinching pennies; it's about making informed decisions that offer the best value for your money. When you break down each element of your travel – from transport and accommodation to food and activities – you'll find that your budget stretches further than you ever thought possible. There are loads of tips and resourceful strategies that our community members and we have personally used to make the most of holidays, days out and travel, all without breaking the bank.

DAYS OUT

There's so much to see and do, especially with the kids, but the costs can add up. Apart from the usual advice like booking tickets in advance or going for family deals, there are some lesser-known tips that can make your day out in the UK more affordable without compromising on the fun.

Take advantage of 2-for-1 deals

Rail companies often offer 2-for-1 entry deals on attractions if you travel by train. You might not see these advertised everywhere, but a quick search online can reveal which places participate in such offers. They're sometimes available on cereal boxes too, around the school holidays.

Make use of loyalty points

You might collect points on your credit card or a store loyalty card and never use them. Some of these can be converted into vouchers for days out at cinemas, zoos and even some amusement parks.

Visit during off-peak hours

Some attractions have cheaper admission fees if you visit late in the afternoon. You may not have the whole day to explore, but a few hours at a reduced price can still be worthwhile. Art galleries are especially good for this, as most kids don't want to spend too long in an art gallery! Some galleries, like the Tate in London, are free entry anyway, but they also run free evening events with live music. You can pop in for an hour and feel like you've had a bit of culture without spending anything.

Get a membership

You can get access to National Trust or English Heritage sites with an annual membership, which could save you a lot of money and give you something different to do with the family every weekend. Some people aren't aware that these memberships often include free parking at many beachside locations, so you could try to get more from the area you visit.

 Skint Tip: *Single parent? Single parents often get a bad deal at visitor attractions. Instead of one-adult family admission prices there's often a single parent 'discount', which effectively means single parents pay more for their entry*

than adults who happen to be in a couple. Shout out to the National Trust and English Heritage, where admission prices for single adults are exactly half of what it costs for two adults, making family days out more affordable for single parents and their families.

Use Park and Ride

In many cities and larger towns, parking in the centre can be expensive. Consider parking in a free or cheaper area and taking public transport into the heart of the action.

Consider a Leisure Pass

Several cities offer a leisure pass that gives access to multiple attractions at a discounted rate. It may seem like an upfront cost, but if you plan to visit multiple sites, it's well worth it.

 Skint Tip: *Saving money on days out is about more than just looking for the obvious discounts. It's about being resourceful, planning ahead and, sometimes, thinking a bit outside the box. These savings strategies invite you to experience the richness of the UK in a financially smart way so you can make the most of every adventure.*

 Skint Tip 2: *Everyone wants to see the big sites like Stonehenge or Edinburgh Castle. But major attractions*

are pricey. The good news is that the UK is filled with lesser-known places that are both cheaper and less crowded. From pleasure gardens and beaches to water mills and animal sanctuaries, a big day out doesn't have to mean big spending. Join local Facebook groups in the area to get tips on how the locals live – the best places to go to (and to avoid) as well as ideas for cheaper days out. Also, you can research online forums and local blogs to discover more hidden gems.

HOLIDAYS

Staycations or holidays abroad?

Deciding between a staycation and going abroad for a holiday can be a bit like choosing between apples and oranges; each has its own appeal and costs. Let's break it down to see what might work best for you.

Staycations

Staycations, where you stay in the UK for your holiday, can offer an alternative that can be quite kind on your wallet if you do it right.

The main and most obvious saving is that you're cutting out hefty airfare costs, and there's no need to worry about currency exchange rates eating into your budget.

Public transport or even a car journey is generally easier to plan when you're not using Google Translate and/or Maps every five minutes. You can also opt for self-catering accommodation, offering you the flexibility to cook your own meals and save on dining out. And make no mistake, the UK is full of beautiful and interesting places to explore. Whether you want picturesque countryside, beautiful beaches or bustling cities, you won't have a problem finding somewhere lovely to rest up for a while.

However, a staycation isn't without its financial pitfalls. Popular UK holiday spots like Cornwall and Kent are always in demand, and prices for accommodation can soar during peak times. Activities and dining out can also add up if you're not careful. But with smart planning and a focus on value for money rather than just the cheapest options, a staycation can be both delightful and economical.

Pros	Cons
Travel: There are no flights or ferry crossings to pay for.	Travel: Train journeys can be expensive and the traffic a nightmare.
Pet-friendly: No need to worry about pet sitters or kennels; your pets can often come along on a staycation.	Weather: The UK isn't exactly known for reliable, sunny weather.

Pros	**Cons**
Less stress: You don't have to navigate foreign languages, cultures or transport systems.	Can you relax?: Sometimes a complete escape is necessary for a real break.
Flexibility: You can be more spontaneous with no flights to catch or strict itineraries.	Day-to-day costs: You might still spend on visiting places like museums, parks or cinemas, which could add up.
No currency exchange: You won't lose money when changing pounds to another currency.	Less exotic: If you're looking for a dramatically different setting or culture, a staycation might not offer that.

Plan ahead

As the idea of a staycation has become more common, especially since the Covid-19 pandemic, we've noticed accommodation gets booked up faster and further in advance. This is especially true if you have someone who needs special access or if you want to take pets, so you need to book earlier. Last-minute deals are still out there, though, and great if you have the flexibility to do things late. If you can book off-peak, avoiding the summer months and school holidays, prices will be even lower. Just check first if the places you want to visit will still be open!

Finding cheap accommodation

We all want to stay somewhere nice on holiday – it's not really a holiday if you're just tolerating somewhere! But even with the boom in peer-to-peer renting and sites like Airbnb, accommodation can be expensive, especially if you're travelling with the family.

Self-catering – renting a house, cottage or an apartment – can often be cheaper than a hotel, and you can make big savings on food by having a kitchen to prepare and cook your own meals. The downside is you have to prepare and cook your own meals! A hotel takes all the strain out of your holiday experience, but prices can be prohibitive. We love the secret hotel feature on Lastminute.com that offers a 'mystery' hotel booking at a fraction of the usual cost. While they are billed as secret destinations, you don't have to be Sherlock Holmes to work out the hotel using some of the details in the description and the wonder of Google.

And if you're fed up with the urban sprawl and want to get back to nature, why not try camping? It's by far the cheapest option for accommodation and many campsites are located in truly breathtaking spots. Being outside, enjoying the fresh air and nature is all entirely free of charge and we know from holidays with our girls that it is the time spent outdoors that they love and remember.

Skint Tip: *Instead of buying new camping gear for yourself, see if there is a Library of Stuff local to you where you can rent out camping kit, or ask to borrow it from a friend or neighbour. The app KitUp also lets you rent outdoor gear from locals.*

Youth hostels are another great way to stay cheaply in some knockout locations. No longer just for youth, many of them have private or family rooms that you won't need to share. You could also try staying in university rooms during the holidays, as some unis rent out their empty rooms on campus at low prices. The website UniversityRooms.com lets you book empty student rooms all over the world. They are generally very basic but many are in great locations for sightseeing and, unlike a lot of hotels, have availability in the school holidays. Home swaps with friends or family living in other parts of the UK can also give you a cost-effective holiday, as you'll only need to arrange to get there.

Another option is to try a farm stay, where you can get free or very low-cost accommodation in exchange for helping with chores such as picking fruit or clearing up after the animals. Woofing – Working On Organic Farms – is now a popular tourist activity all over the world, and a great learning experience. Check out WWOOF.org.uk.

Transport

Getting to where you want to go can start to eat into your budget, particularly if you are not driving. A Railcard can get you big discounts on family rail travel (and if you've been collecting your loyalty points you might be able to get one for free). Instead of buying a train ticket for your entire journey, you can sometimes save money by splitting the journey into parts and buying separate tickets for each leg. Some sites like Trainline.com will help you work out the cheapest options, saving you time as well. If there are four or five of you travelling together, a taxi might work out cheaper, so find out the prices ahead of time to see what's better value. Once you're there, many UK towns and cities have bike-share and e-scooter schemes. It's often cheaper and more enjoyable than other forms of public transport.

Activities

The UK is filled with free museums, parks and historical sites – you just have to do the research first, and there are plenty of blogs with information as well as local council websites. We are spoilt for choice for outdoor fun, with nature reserves, beaches and hiking trails offering great experiences at little to no cost.

 Skint Fave: *Something the Skints love to do as a family is geocaching. It's treasure hunting done using a GPS-enabled device (your phone). You get to explore little-known areas on the hunt for a hidden cache. Some can be tiny, like a 33mm camera film case; but we've found some huge old ammo boxes in the past, too! It's such a fun thing to do for adults*

and children as you have to work together as a team. Again, being outside and spending time together comes without a charge and is the stuff of memories that last.

Food and dining

Eating out is one of the great pleasures of any holiday but the costs can mount up. For daytime eats it's usually pretty easy to pack a picnic, which can save on the cost of fast food or a sit-down meal. It doesn't need to be fancy. Find out about local markets, away from other tourists and supermarkets, where you can find fresh, affordable produce. You'll eat like a local and save money at the same time. If you do want to eat out, use Facebook and local news sites to find recommendations. Most independent restaurants do cheap eats and special offers, especially during holiday season; it's just about plugging into the local network rather than going for another Pizza Express. Although if you've got your Tastecard with you, that can also be a good option!

What else?

Make sure to take advantage of any cashback or coupons where you can. Even if you travel last minute, booking online the day before for an activity can be cheaper than booking on the door. Travel insurance doesn't just cover you for trips abroad but can help with the costs of lost or stolen cash or luggage even in the UK.

Holidays abroad

Holidays abroad offer a thrilling escape filled with new cultures and landscapes but often come with a higher price tag. However, as always, some smart planning can make an overseas adventure more budget-friendly. From booking flights in advance and travelling in the off-season to choosing destinations where your money stretches further, there are ways to save without skimping on the experience. But be cautious: costs like travel insurance, snacks at the airport, visas and even vaccinations can sneak up on you. While the cost is usually higher than a staycation, careful budgeting and smart choices can make a holiday abroad a rewarding experience that doesn't break the bank.

Pros	Cons
New experiences: Different cultures, foods, and sights can be exciting.	Travel fatigue: Long flights and jet lag can take their toll, eating into your actual holiday time.
Package deals: Sometimes all-inclusive holidays can offer value for money, covering food, accommodation and even some activities.	Hidden costs: As well as travel insurance, and the potential for costly visas, you may also need to factor in costs for car seat hire, airport transfers, and potentially new suitable clothing.

Pros	Cons
Weather: Want guaranteed sun or prefer snowy slopes? Going abroad provides a range of weather options.	Language barriers: Not speaking the local language can be a challenge and could limit your experience.
Cultural enrichment: The opportunity to immerse yourself in a new culture can be a transformative experience.	Health risks: Depending on the destination, there might be a risk of diseases or health conditions you must prepare for. Vaccinations can also be expensive.

If you're planning a holiday abroad here are some ways to save money:

Flights and travel

You'll often find the best flight prices several months before your planned trip, so book in advance where possible. While package holidays come with their perks of ease of booking and usually ATOL/ABTA travel protection, we've often saved money when travelling by booking the flights and accommodation separately. Use flight comparison sites such as Skyscanner and Google Flights to help you find the cheapest flights across multiple airlines. Then book directly with a hotel or other accommodation. This saves on fees you could otherwise pay to booking companies.

Most airlines now add options for sitting in a certain aisle, getting on the plane first and even taking luggage on board. We say why skip the queue and pay for fast track when it just means sitting on the airplane longer? And if the adults can't always sit together does it really matter? You're about to spend a whole holiday together! You can avoid the added costs of checking your luggage in with smart packing. We have come to enjoy the challenge of packing light and avoiding those fees. It makes you really think about what you need (very little, it turns out) and it's amazing how much you can actually fit in cabin luggage. Most airports have a pharmacy in Departures, where you can pick up larger toiletries that can't get through security or bulky nappies (and take them as extra carry on). If you're extra organised, you can buy what you need and do Click and Collect to make sure the products are there before you fly. How good is that?

Accommodation

As with staying in the UK, you have many options, from hotels to private rental flats to villas and houses. Booking direct is always the cheapest option. If your hotel is part of a chain it might be worth looking into loyalty schemes and membership programmes, as you can sometimes get money off for signing up, especially if there's a newsletter to receive.

Activities

Walking tours are a great way to see a place and many cities offer 'pay-what-you-feel' walking tours. Even cheaper, you can find walking tours online that you can print out or follow from your phone. The City Map app is free and helps you get around easily and provides suggested routes. Hop-on, hop-off sightseeing buses offer great value for getting around a city, and if you plan your day and have a few places you want to see they can work out far cheaper than taxis or public transport. If you're heading for the coast or countryside, use the regional tourist information service to find deals and discounts. Google Earth is also a great way to get your bearings and spot off-the-beaten track places and remote beaches. You can avoid expensive beach clubs and sunbeds by embracing the wild-swimming movement! The Wild Swimming website lists rivers, lakes and waterfalls around the world where the swimming is free and in beautiful settings. Don't forget to pack a picnic.

 Skint Tip: *Learning basic phrases can help you get a better deal. Use Google Translate and you don't even need to buy a phrasebook. Pop in what you want to say, and it will translate it for you. If you're stuck with road signs, you can take a photo and the translator will tell you what it means, without needing to type anything in.*

Food and drink

All-inclusive is generally a very budget-friendly option and great if you've got a family to feed and don't mind staying in the same place. But if you want to get out and about without breaking the bank, it's really about eating like a local. Take a step back from the main strips and seafront locations and seek out the smaller places where in-the-know locals eat. Prices are generally lower as they want the locals to keep coming back, rather than a tourist who'll only eat there once. Also, find a market to try local street food. It's a cheap and tasty way to sample local cuisine.

 Skint Tip: *Let go of preconceptions about what eating out should be like. Often the simplest location and most modest food is the tastiest. We love the chicken restaurants in Portugal where the TV is always on and the wine is always home-made. It feels like being in someone's front room. The food is just delicious and extremely good value.*

Transport

Buses, trams and trains are generally cheaper than taxis or car hires. If you are in a very touristy area, buses will usually stop very near to attractions so they're worth using. Some cities offer city passes, including unlimited public transport and entry to various attractions. E-scooters and bikes, and even roller-skates, can all be hired cheaply and make getting around part of the fun.

Saving money on your money

If you are with a high-street bank, the exchange rate you pay may be higher than some internet-only banks. There are online comparison tables to show the best and cheapest card to use, depending on where you travel. If you are planning to haggle, cash is always king and you can likely get a better discount if you let your vendor know you've got cash.

 Skint Tip: *If you use a card to pay for things abroad, you should always choose to pay in the local currency, rather than in pounds. You will then pay the actual exchange rate, rather than a higher rate created by the vendor (which usually has a fee added on top).*

So, is it cheaper to have a staycation or go abroad? It really depends on various factors like the time of year, what activities you plan to do and what you want from your holiday. Sometimes a staycation could turn out to be just as expensive as going abroad, especially if you plan lots of activities or dine out often.

The key is to plan well and do research into where you're planning to go, consider what you really want from your break, and make informed choices that allow you to get the most value – both financially and emotionally – from your time off.

Still Feel Too Skint To Save?

By now, if you've taken some of our frugal living tips on board, done the Thirty-day No Eating Out Challenge and started meal planning like a pro, you might be feeling a little bit less broke. Still, we know that when you're on the breadline, having anything left over to save can seem like an impossible dream.

Back when we began our money-saving journey, I remember hearing about the 52-week saving challenge. This is where you save an increasing amount each week, starting with £1 in the first week of January and finishing with £52 in the last week of December. This method helps you raise £1,378 over the year – an amount not to be sniffed at. But for us, the idea of being able to save £52 in the last week of December just always seemed a bit too far out of reach!

Still, Skint Mum and I liked the idea of using a fun challenge to motivate ourselves and have some money put aside, even if it wasn't quite in the thousands. So we created the 1p Saving Challenge instead.

As you've probably guessed, instead of £1 a week, you save 1p a day and increase it daily by 1p. So it's 1p on day one, 2p on day two and you keep going until the last day when you should be able to save £3.65. (One of those piggy boxes that requires a tin opener to get it open is a big help here so that you can't dip into the fund if you need some cash.)

By the end of the year, you will have saved £667.95 – still a really decent amount (enough to pay for Christmas) and all starting with just 1p.

 Skint Tip: *Lots of people do this at the start of January but you can start it any time of year. It's great for when you have something special to save for, like a holiday. Starting at the beginning of the school summer holidays means you'll have a really decent pot of spending money at the start of the next summer holidays. You could also do it in reverse, so you start by saving £3.65 on day one and save 1p less each day! By the time it comes to the last day, saving 1p will feel like a breeze.*

Part Two

MAKE MONEY

If our story tells us all one thing about financial well-being in the twenty-first century, it's that having a job isn't always enough. If you're like us, you probably grew up believing that if you got a decent job and worked hard you'd be all right in life. But for so many of us these days, that idea is basically a fairy tale. While our parents and grandparents might have owned their own homes, had two cars and regular holidays, often on one income, that simply isn't the case for our generation, or for the ones that have followed. And while some might think that Millennials are all spending too much on avocados and flat whites, the fact is that many of us can't afford our lives even on two incomes. We don't need to go into the whys and wherefores of how this has happened: the global economy, privatisation, climate change and wars have all played their part. But we're not here to talk about politics or fiscal policy, we just want to have a nice life.

So what's the solution to this problem? Obviously saving money is key and hopefully you've started to put some of the ideas from Part One into practice and you're seeing the results. But it's not all about watching what's going out; ideally, you want to also be increasing what's coming in.

Get both those things right and you're well on your way to not being skint (we never said it was rocket science!). So, this part of our book is all about introducing a little extra to your bottom line, with side hustles and second revenue streams; finding new ways to earn that booster, on top of your wages if you are an employee or as well as your existing income if you are self-employed. We'll also look at how you can get the most out of the job you already have, from asking for a pay rise to maximising the subsidies and benefits you might not even know you are entitled to. We'll also look at how being smarter with your banking can create extra wealth, and give you a few tips about setting up a new venture by yourself, no matter how big or small.

At the end of the day, we can't tell you how much extra you need to make or guarantee the amounts that some of our ideas will pay out. But we can say with certainty that they will all help you earn more than you do right now, without requiring you to give up entirely on a life outside work – and that is what we are all about!

6

MAKE YOUR JOB
WORK FOR YOU

I f like 77 per cent of the working-age population you are in a full-time job, you might reasonably assume that because you work all week and take home a monthly salary, the only way you can make a bit extra is with a side hustle or an extra income stream. These things are certainly going to help and we'll talk about the best ones for you shortly. But before that, we want you to think about the job you already have and work out if you are really maximising its earning potential. Sounds interesting, right?

To be clear, this isn't about going for that promotion or getting a new job somewhere else – although if you want those things you should totally go for it. But we can't give you career advice. What we can tell you, though, is that there are a number of ways you can boost your income from work, without changing jobs or taking on loads of extra responsibilities. You just need to know how.

ASKING FOR A PAY RISE

If you're already employed but finding that your earnings aren't covering the basics, it can rarely do any harm to ask for a pay rise. Many companies offer performance reviews and automatic pay rises in line with inflation. But often there is scope to ask for more! You just have to know how to do it. For many people, the thought of asking for extra money in your wage packet can seem daunting, and there's always a worry that you will upset your boss or appear somehow greedy by asking. But remember that finding and keeping good staff is a major burden for employers and most will want to keep hold of good staff if they can. Bosses are also busy people; they might need a nudge to take notice of you! Here are some hints to help you seal the deal:

- Request a real-life meeting with your boss, rather than emailing. This is an important moment; don't hide behind emails.
- Time it right. If you've done something over and

above your job description and you know your boss is impressed with you, this is the perfect time to ask for that rise. If you haven't been pulling your weight recently, it's probably not a good time to ask.

- Fix up, look sharp. Dressing for success is a thing! You might be at the bottom of the ladder in the office, but psychologists have proved that if you dress like a manager, you'll start to feel and act more like one. Now is the time to hold your head high and present your best self at work.

- Be realistic and ask for something you think they can reasonably afford to give you. Research average salaries for your role online and ask people you know who will give you an honest answer.

- If they can't help you now, find out if and when you might be likely to get a rise. Knowing a little extra is on the way can be very helpful when planning your finances.

- If you feel nervous about what you're going to say, write it down and have a little practice with a friend or in the mirror before you go in.

CUTTING THE COST OF YOUR COMMUTE

Travel to work can be crazy expensive. As we explained earlier, it was the huge cost of commuting to London every day that was the straw that broke the camel's back for Mr Skint and started us off on the Skint Dad blog. We know just how demotivating it is to have to spend such a big chunk of your earnings on simply travelling to work. Not to mention the negative impact it has on your well-being, whether you're on a crowded train or sat bumper to bumper on the M25, a busy commute is not something many people really enjoy. Plus, the temptation to buy coffees and breakfast on the way in is all too real! The whole thing can end up costing you way more than you should be spending on getting to work. So, how do you tip the scales in your favour?

1. Firstly, take a minute to review the costs of your journey to work and write it all down. Petrol, train fares, coffees, parking, bus fares; the whole lot. Looking at it as one total figure, rather than a series of small incidental costs, can be quite a shock, but it can also inspire you to do something. Where can you make savings? Could you walk the bus part of your journey? Can you quit your morning Costa habit? Visualise the savings by including them in your budget and see how your income increases.

2. Ask your employer about Cycle to Work schemes. With these schemes you can buy new cycling equipment and have the costs taken tax efficiently from your wages, so you don't have to pay big upfront costs. You can also rent bikes if you don't want to buy one. You dodge all those nasty parking fees and train fares. Plus, cycling to work has the obvious benefit of being a healthy choice and can save you money on gym fees and exercise classes. Winner!

3. Employee car share schemes are a brilliant way to keep the costs of petrol and parking down. Research in 2016 found that the average annual saving made by someone car sharing every day was over £1,000! Ask around at work for details; if there isn't one already set up, you know what you need to do. 'Closed-loop' work-based carpools (i.e. a group of people with a common destination or location, not open to the public) are increasingly common and in some places there are now 2+ people lanes for cars, giving you priority over those poor old lone drivers wasting all their cash on petrol for one. Most importantly, lift sharing can buy you extra time in the morning and that, as we know, is priceless.

4. Push for more home working. Since the Covid-19 pandemic we've all been working at home a lot more. It will depend on your work and your

employer, but if working from home is a possibility for you, it is always worth asking if you can do some more hours from home. Even if you do just one day at home a week, you will save on travel costs and food on the go. You can also claim from HMRC for some expenses such as heating and electricity if you are working from home. Add up your savings from home working and put the money into a savings pot for a holiday or Christmas.

CHECK YOUR CHILDCARE ENTITLEMENTS

Let's talk about something important for parents who work: childcare entitlements! If you're a working parent or carer in England, you should know that you're not alone when it comes to sorting out care for your little ones. There are different ways the government can help you pay for childcare.

One big helper is Tax-Free Childcare. With this, for every £8 you pop into a special account to pay for childcare, the government adds an extra £2. It's not just for nurseries or childminders; you can also use it for after-school clubs to help with wrap-around care. That's like getting free money!

Lastly, don't forget about free nursery hours. Kids between the ages of three and four can get up to thirty free hours of nursery each week during term time. That's a good chunk of time that you don't have to worry about paying for.

So, if you're working and need to sort childcare, look into these options. They could save you a lot of money and stress. Speak to your boss, check government websites, or even chat with other parents to find out more. Every penny saved on childcare is a penny you can use somewhere else!

7

SIDE HUSTLES

Talking about your side hustle has become a popular online trend in recent years and it seems like everyone on Instagram is earning extra, or so-called 'passive', income from some scheme or another. But are all the influencers for real? Are side hustles really that simple to do? And how do you decide what the best one is for you?

The good news from Skint HQ is that yes, you can earn extra cash from the comfort of your sofa and there are literally hundreds of ways you can do this – we know because we do it! But some side hustles are better than others and you have to weigh up the pros and cons. There is no such thing as a free school lunch, and even the cleverest side hustle will require some of your time and effort. It's easy to start out enthusiastically, but if you're already working full time and coming home tired and the income you're getting from your side hustle isn't that much, you're going to lose interest pretty quickly.

Passive income is another buzzword on social media. It really just refers to the earnings you make from something that may have initially required a bit of effort but now generally pays out automatically, like renting out something you own or publishing an online course. Or it can be income you earn while you're doing something else that you'd be doing anyway, like entering competitions while watching TV.

Whatever you decide to hustle on the side, we've learned that the key to creating a lucrative passive revenue stream that you will stick at is to do something that matches your interests and skills, and ideally something that, if it became successful enough, you would enjoy doing full time. The Skint Dad blog is a very real example of a side hustle that became a full-time career. We wouldn't have put so much time and care into the blog in the early days if it wasn't something we both enjoyed doing. When it became clear it might be something we could do full time, there was never any question that we'd want to do it because we both enjoyed it so much.

If you're not sure yet what kind of side hustle might work for you, don't worry. We've put together a list of all the main areas of opportunity, including the pros and cons, to help you decide what the best side hustle for you would be.

SKINT DAD'S TOP SIDE HUSTLES AND HOW TO DO THEM

1. **Sell your old clothes and books.** Hands up if your cupboards are full of clothes you never wear or your loft is packed with boxes of items you never use. We've all got too much stuff! The good news is that someone out there wants that old trike in your porch or that mohair jumper from the eighties that's hanging in your wardrobe. Most of us have been selling our unwanted things on eBay for a while, but there are now lots of other more targeted apps where you can sell your stuff. Vinted and Depop are great for second-hand clothes, and there's Ziffit for CDs, DVDs, console games and books. New apps and online communities are springing up all the time. Do a bit of research and find out where the best place to sell your stuff is. Then set aside some time, maybe each day or week, to devote to selling your unwanted items. You can do it while you're watching TV or listening to a podcast, or when you've got the kids at home. You'll be amazed at how it all adds up and you'll love the space it makes at home! If you don't want to sell online, you can still sell stuff at a local car boot sale or auction house. Just try not to come home with more stuff than you went with!

Pros: No big outlay on stock, just head to your wardrobe.

Cons: Your supply of stock is probably finite, so at some point you'll need to buy more to sell more.

2. **Rent out your stuff.** The sharing economy is here to stay! What's the sharing economy? It's basically the model that companies like Airbnb and Uber are based on. People can share their resources, sometimes for free but often for a fee, with other people online. You can rent out your car when you're not using it on Turo.com. If you've got designer clothes, hats and shoes gathering dust there are specialist rental apps like By Rotation, but main retailers like Asos and Marks and Spencer are also cottoning on to the rental game. You can even rent out your tent and camping gear! (Head to KitUp or Fat Llama.) It's a great way to get your existing resources working for you when they're not being used.

Pros: Relatively easy money for something you already own.

Cons: Items will require maintenance and you need to keep your reviews up to stay in the game.

3. **Rent out your space.** If you are lucky enough to have some extra space at home that you don't need, you can earn extra money by renting it out. You can rent out your spare room to a lodger (try SpareRoom, Gumtree or MondaytoFriday) and the government will give you a tax break of up to £7,500 under its Rent a Room scheme. If you earn over that from the rent you make you can still claim expenses; it's a great way to boost your income! If you don't have a spare room but you have outdoor space, you can rent out your drive-way to commuters (JustPark) or if you have a bit of storage space you can charge people to keep their stuff safe via Storemates.com.

 Skint Tip: *If you live somewhere that other people like to visit for their holidays, or even if you don't but you have a lovely home and enjoy meeting new people, you can list your home on Airbnb or similar home-rental sites. The Airbnb bubble may have burst a bit as the marketplace became flooded with substandard rentals, but there is still demand for good, authentic home stays. If you are the kind of person who loves to make your home look nice or you have a quirky space in a sought-after destination, it's definitely worth giving it a go. The only downside is you need to find somewhere else to live while your guests are staying in your home!*

4. **Earn money for your pictures.** Are you always taking photographs? Do you get lots of likes for your images on social media? You could sell your photos and earn money just from the pictures in your camera roll! Stock image libraries like Shutterstock and Istockphoto let you upload your pics to their library. Then when someone uses your photos you get a fee. It might only be small amounts to begin with but over time and with the right pictures, you could earn a pretty penny.

   Pros: You're already taking pictures; you might as well get paid for them!
   Cons: You'll probably earn pennies to begin with – this is a long game.

5. **Start your own YouTube channel.** You might think of YouTube as somewhere to watch prank videos or catch up on the latest cute cat content, but have you ever considered that the people making the videos and putting them out there are making quite a lot of money? Being a YouTuber is a serious business! You'll need to create videos that people want to watch, and get at least 1,000 followers before you can start earning money for your content. But once you're up and running you will be paid every time someone watches your videos. To keep this kind of

thing in the genuine side hustle zone try to make videos about something you love doing or you're already doing for fun, like art, applying make-up, or organising your home. It might sound bizarre but people love watching this stuff!

> **Pros:** Easy to start and set-up costs can be low.
> **Cons:** You need to keep making good content to grow your audience, so it can be time-consuming.

6. **Monetise something you're already doing.** We've already talked about being a childminder if you're at home with young kids. But if eating out is your thing how about becoming a mystery diner? Or if you've got a dog, you could become a dog-walker. If crafting is your hobby, try setting up a shop on Etsy and see if you can sell your work. Love to bake? Get a food hygiene certificate and you can sell your cakes and loaves to local cafés and restaurants. Even if you have no hobbies and your favourite thing to do is simply shopping, sites like Quidco and TopCashback will give you money back for shopping online via their sites. The idea here is to start earning money for something you're already doing.

Pros: You don't need to step too far out of your comfort zone to make this happen.
Cons: It could take the fun out of your hobby or pastime.

7. **Complete online surveys.** Companies and brands are always looking for quick ways to get customer opinions on new products or services. It's not exactly fun but it is easy to fill out surveys and you can do it from your phone while watching television or if you have a spare five minutes. Head to sites like YouGov, Swagbucks and LifePoints and you can earn cash or gift cards for your favourite stores.

Pros: Can be done while you're watching TV.
Cons: You need to do quite a few surveys to earn significant amounts.

Case Study

Sally is a support worker and, with her husband, manages her money well enough to be able to pay their bills, and put away some savings for retirement. But there's rarely enough left over for treats or holidays, so Sally does a little side hustle to raise some extra cash. A few times a week, she logs in to survey sites to answer polls and questions. With a full-time job she doesn't have a lot of time to devote to it, so she does it while having a cup of tea in the morning or watching TV in the evening. Sally averages earnings of around £80 a month and believes she could make more if she joined more sites and did more surveys. But for now, she wants to keep her earnings under the Trading Allowance, so she doesn't need to pay tax.

8. **Write an online course.** Are you an expert on a certain subject? Do you know everything there is to know about something that you think other people might be interested in? It could be something obscure like growing mushrooms or it could be something with broad appeal like crochet. Whatever your specialist subject is, you can turn your knowledge into a course that people can buy online. Online learning is a massive growth area and people are embracing the idea of learning at home in their own time, so if you've got the knowledge get out there and share it! Sites like Shopify and Wix offer great support for anyone who wants to write their own course.

   Pros: You'll earn a fee every time someone downloads your course.

Cons: Quite a lot of work upfront to write the course and set it up.

9. **Host international students and actors.** If you've got a spare room and you're not already using SpareRoom to let it out, you could consider hosting international students and/or travelling actors and performers. This is a great option for those who don't want to have people in their home all the time but don't mind doing it occasionally. Contact your local language school and/or theatres to find out about becoming a host.

   Pros: Good money and you can meet interesting people.
   Cons: You'll have a lodger in your home!

10. **Become an affiliate marketer.** Have you ever bought something online after watching someone make a recommendation about it? This is what's called affiliate marketing and it's a great way to make your social media activity start to pay out! With affiliate marketing you use your social media platform (e.g. your Instagram account or Facebook page) to advertise someone else's products or services and you earn a commission if and when they sell something via your referral link or code. Affiliate marketing is especially effective

the more followers you have, so if you have a podcast, are an influencer or have an online store of your own, growing your audience will grow your potential for sales. This is perhaps the ultimate in passive income and that is why we love it!

Pros: Earns you money while you sleep.
Cons: You have to let your followers know you're posting an ad and will make money if they purchase via your link.

The Skint Dad step-by-step guide to affiliate marketing

Step 1: Choose a niche

First, decide what you want to focus on. This should be something you know a bit about and are interested in. It should also align with the audience you are planning to share with. If you love cooking, focus on that, or even on kitchen gadgets.

Step 2: Research affiliate programmes

Look for companies or online platforms that offer affiliate programmes in your chosen area. Websites like Amazon Associates or Awin are great starting points in the UK.

Step 3: Sign up

Once you pick a programme, fill in their application form. They might ask you for some details and will give you a unique link that tracks if sales come from you.

Step 4: Create quality content

To get people to click your link, you need to offer them something valuable. Write helpful blog posts, social media captions, make videos or share tips that are related to the product you're promoting. Try to make the content informative and make sure your affiliate links are included naturally.

Step 5: Share and promote your link

Now comes the fun part. Share this special link on your blog, social media, or wherever you can, including forums related to your niche and other online communities. But remember, always let people know it's an affiliate link so you're being transparent and following the Advertising Standards Authority (ASA) regulations.

Step 6: Track and improve

Most affiliate programmes give you a way to see how many clicks and sales you've made on a dashboard. Check this regularly and think about ways you could tweak and develop what you're doing.

Step 7: Get paid!

When someone clicks your link and buys something, you get paid a commission. Each programme has its own rules for how and when they pay, so make sure to check that out.

There you go, a simple guide to affiliate marketing in the UK. It takes some effort to start, but once you're up and running, it can be a brilliant way to make some extra money!

11. **Refer a friend.** Sending a referral code to a friend when you buy something is a great way of getting free cash. Referring to friends and family is a quick and easy method of gaining free

money, and it involves very little effort. We find some of the best referral links usually come from energy companies, banks and broadband providers. Get into the habit of doing it and make it part of your online shopping process.

Pros: It's free money!
Cons: You have to wait until your friend signs up before you can get your payout.

12. **Become a comper.** We're not talking about doing the National Lottery, which actually costs you money and rarely pays out. We're talking about competitions that are free to enter and in many cases offer some pretty astounding prizes, including free cash.

There are literally thousands of competitions running every day, week and month in the UK. You could go all out and enter 100 a week, but we reckon more manageable is somewhere around thirty competitions a week, in order to guarantee at least some prize payback. Free lotteries such as the Pick My Postcode are great. You'll need to check the results daily to see if you've won a share of £800, but it's definitely worth a few seconds of your time.

Pros: Free to enter.

Cons: You need to make a decent amount of entries to win, unless you're very lucky.

13. **Scan your receipts.** This has to be one of the least likely but simplest ways to earn a bit of extra cash. We like to keep our receipts anyway as it helps us budget, but if you're someone who generally chucks your receipts away you might want to reconsider as keeping them and taking a picture of them can actually earn you free cash!

   Receipt-scanning apps like Storewards, Shoppix and Amazon Shopper Panel pay you to upload copies of your receipts for any purchase from any shop. You don't get paid actual cash for your receipts but you do earn tokens whenever you make a submission and once you've made enough you can get a payout or a voucher for Amazon, which is kind of like free money in our book. The data collected is analysed and used by the companies for market research purposes. They use it to see shopping habits of the general population to help retailers with business decisions.

   It may take you a while to build up enough tokens for a payout or voucher, but there's really very little effort required and it has the added bonus of helping you stay aware of what you're spending. And if you're self-employed, it's a great way of keeping track of your expenses. At the end of the day, being given a receipt is something that's already happening, you might as well make some money out of it! Side-hustle gold!

Pros: Takes seconds to do.
Cons: Building up points can take a while and a lot of receipts.

Fancy a spot of wombling?

You can take your receipt scanning to a whole new level and be a womble. Womblers collect receipts other people have left behind – usually in the supermarket – and scan them in at the same time as their own receipts. There are a surprising amount of old, unwanted receipts lying around in shops, and taking a few seconds to scan them in and upload them can really boost your balance. What have you got to lose? Do check the terms of the apps and sites you use to make sure they accept wombled receipts.

---

14. **Become a drop shipper.** Drop shipping is an exciting side hustle that lets you sell products without ever having to touch them. Imagine

this: you set up an online shop and list various products. But instead of buying and storing these items yourself, you work with suppliers who hold the stock. When someone buys from your shop, the supplier sends the item directly to the customer. You're like the middleman, connecting buyers to products.

The beauty of drop shipping is that you don't need to worry about stock, storage or postage. Your main focus is on building a great online shop and/or social media presence and attracting customers. You can choose to sell anything you like, from fashion and tech gadgets to pet supplies. The key is to find a niche that's popular but not too crowded with competitors.

Now, while the start-up costs for drop shipping are relatively low, it's not entirely without challenges. You need to find reliable suppliers, set prices that are competitive but also profitable for you. You'll likely spend a good amount of time on customer service, dealing with queries or issues that may arise.

Despite the challenges, if done right, drop shipping can be a profitable and flexible side hustle. It allows you to dip your toes into the world of retail without a huge investment, and you can run it from the comfort of your own home (without needing to make any space in a spare room for stock). So, if you have a knack for spotting trends and a willingness to learn the ropes of e-commerce, drop shipping could be your ticket to a profitable side hustle.

Pros: Makes buying and selling easy.
Cons: Setting up can be complicated.

15. **Flog your old phones and tech.** Selling old phones and tech is a fantastic way to declutter and make some extra money at the same time. We all have that drawer or cupboard filled with gadgets we no longer use. Instead of letting them gather dust, why not turn them into cash? Old smartphones, tablets, laptops and even game consoles can fetch a decent price if they're in good working condition.

It's a win-win situation. You get rid of items you don't need, someone else gets the tech they've been looking for at a reduced price, and you walk away with extra money in your pocket.

The process is quite simple. Various online platforms and shops specialise in buying used tech. You can also go the DIY route and sell directly to buyers through social media marketplaces or auction sites like eBay. Either way, you'll need to describe your items accurately and maybe upload some photos. Don't forget to wipe all personal data from your devices before selling them; you don't want your personal information ending up in the wrong hands!

Skint Tip: *Be careful selling higher priced items on market-places, particularly if they offer to pay by PayPal and pay extra for you to arrange a courier. This is a well-known scam and can see you lose your item and the money. If you're ever unsure or it doesn't feel right, ask a friend or come and talk with the Skints and members of our community to double check.*

Pros: Readily available stock.
Cons: You could lose important photos or information.

16. **Sell on rare coins you'll find in your change.** If you've got a sharp eye and a bit of patience, making money by selling rare coins you find in your change could be an excellent side hustle. Believe it or not, there are coins out there in everyday circulation that are worth more than their face value. Collectors are willing to pay a pretty penny for these, and you might just find one mixed in with your loose change.

You might be wondering what makes a coin rare. It could be a special design, an error made during the minting process, or even a limited-edition circulation. Once you find a potentially valuable coin, you can check its worth online. Then, you can sell it through various platforms like auction websites or social media groups dedicated to coin collecting, or directly to a collector.

A few examples of 50p coins that are worth more than their face value are:

1. **Kew Gardens 50p:** Issued in 2009 to commemorate the 250th anniversary of the Royal Botanic Gardens in Kew, this coin is one of the most sought after. It features the famous pagoda from the gardens. You could get around £100 to £200.

2. **2012 Olympic Games 50p:** To celebrate the London 2012 Olympics, a series of 50p coins featuring different sports were released. Some, like the ones featuring football, wrestling or judo are rarer and can fetch a higher price (currently up to £20).

3. **Peter Rabbit 50p:** Beatrix Potter's beloved character has appeared on various 50p coins. Some editions, especially the coloured versions, are highly collectible. The 2018 version had a circulation of just 1.4 million and is currently worth around £10.

Pros: Doesn't require a big investment or a lot of space.

Cons: Relies on luck.

SIDE HUSTLE OR SECOND JOB?

There is often a bit of a grey area between a side hustle and a second job. Still, there are some second jobs that you can do in your own time, and fit in around your already busy life and work. While they require a level of effort and in some cases equipment or skills that mean they're not the kind of side hustles that create entirely passive income from your sofa, they are definitely worth looking into if you want to boost your income and you're prepared to put in the effort. Importantly, they're usually the kind of things you can do under your own steam and therefore can pave the way to setting up your own business and even being self-employed. Here are a few ideas below to get you started.

Transcribing

Transcribing is a brilliant way to make some extra money if you're a quick typist and have a keen ear. What's transcribing, you ask? Well, it's simply changing spoken words into written text. This skill is in high demand in various sectors like legal, medical and entertainment industries.

You could be transcribing interviews, podcasts or even court hearings.

One of the best things about being a transcriber is the flexibility it offers. You can often work from home and choose hours that suit you, making it a great side hustle for busy people. Plus, getting started doesn't require a huge investment. A decent pair of headphones and a computer are often all you need. Some people invest in specialised transcription software, but it's not always necessary.

The pay varies, usually based on the length and complexity of the audio. So, you might earn more for transcribing technical medical interviews compared to straightforward podcasts. It's also a skill that gets easier and faster with practice, meaning you could earn more as you gain experience.

Online customer service

Working in online customer service from the comfort of your home can be a fantastic second job or even become a full-time one. It's a role that's become increasingly popular, especially since many businesses are moving their customer services online. You'll be tasked with answering customer queries, solving problems and making sure people have a good experience when dealing with the company you represent. The job could involve chatting with customers through a messaging service, responding to emails or even handling phone calls.

One of the best things about this role is its flexibility. Many companies offer various shifts, allowing you to fit work around your main job or other commitments. All you really need is a reliable internet connection, a computer, a fixed landline phone line and a quiet space to work. Companies such as Sensée (employed) or Arise (self-employed) regularly look for new people.

 Skint Tip: *If you see a job posted online that seems too good to be true, offering huge pay for very few hours, it's likely not what you hope it would be.*

Home organising

Do you like to keep things tidy in your home? Have you got the bug from watching others do the same on TikTok? Organising spaces in rooms or cupboards has become even more popular thanks to trends on social media platforms. Videos about cleaning hacks, decluttering and keeping tidy have sparked interest in professional home organisation services. If you're good at organising and enjoy transforming cluttered spaces into havens of order, this could be a fantastic side hustle for you to help people who don't have time. Plus, because of the TikTok trend, people are more aware of the value of an organised home, making it easier to attract clients.

What makes this side hustle even more interesting is the opportunity to double up on income. While you're organising someone's wardrobe or kitchen, you could film the process (with the client's permission, of course) and share it on your own social media channels. This could not only attract more clients but also open the door to a second stream of income through social media monetisation, brand collaborations or even tips and donations from viewers who find your content useful.

So, if you've got a knack for creating tidy, functional spaces and you're social media savvy, running a home organisation business is not just a way to make extra money; it's also a chance to ride the wave of a popular trend and maybe even become an internet star in your own right.

Flipping return pallets and lost luggage

Flipping return pallets, lost luggage or other stock is like treasure hunting for profit. People and businesses return items that end up being sold in bulk, often at a fraction of their original price. The same goes for lost luggage that's never claimed. You can buy these items and resell them for a tidy profit. It's a bit like having a second-hand shop, but without needing a physical store.

This side hustle requires a keen eye for value and a knack for selling. You'll need to sift through a mixed bag of goods, figuring out what can be sold as is, what needs a bit of TLC and what's only good for parts or recycling. The thrill is in the hunt and the satisfaction of turning something unwanted into a treasure for someone else.

In terms of investment, you'll need some initial cash to buy your first batch of items, plus a place to store them. But if you do it right, the profits can quickly cover your costs and generate extra cash.

Being an Amazon driver

Being an Amazon driver can be a good way to make some extra cash. Think about it: people are always ordering stuff online, right? So, there's a constant demand for drivers to deliver these packages. This is a job that has you out and about, so it's great if you enjoy being on the move and don't fancy being stuck behind a desk.

You can often choose your hours, so it's easier to fit the work around your other commitments, although you do have targets to meet and can't simply stop if you've not finished deliveries. You'll need a decent car and a clean driving record, of course. Some people worry about fuel costs, but these are generally balanced out by the earnings.

Online tutoring

Online tutoring is an excellent way to share your expertise and make extra cash, all from the comfort of your home. Whether it's maths, English, science, or even a musical instrument, if you've got a skill or subject you excel in, there's likely someone out there eager to learn. Online tutoring has gained a lot of traction, especially with more families looking for extra educational support outside the classroom. And, as you can do it online, the world is your oyster, with the chance to teach people globally. It's a win-win situation: students get the help they need, and you get paid for your knowledge and time.

What makes online tutoring even more appealing is its flexibility. You can set your own hours, allowing you to work around your main job or other responsibilities. All you need is a stable internet connection, a computer with a webcam, and the appropriate software for video calls. Plus, being an online tutor can be rewarding in more ways than one. Not only do you earn money, but you also get the satisfaction of helping someone achieve their academic goals.

Pet sitter

Being a pet sitter can be a dream job for animal lovers looking to make extra money. Imagine getting paid to hang out with adorable cats, dogs or even bunnies! As a pet sitter, you're entrusted with the care of other people's furry (or feathery or scaly) family members while they're away or out for long hours during the day. You might be asked to feed them, walk them, give medication, just provide some good old-fashioned companionship, and perhaps even water the plants while you're there. This is a service that's always in demand, especially during holiday seasons or weekends, when people are more likely to travel.

The best part is you don't need an office or any fancy equipment. Your client's home is your workplace, and often they'll provide all the supplies you need. However, as you'll be alone (and even have their keys), it would be wise to obtain a DBS check to show that you are trustworthy. You can promote your services through social media, word-of-mouth or community boards, making it easy to get started.

Ironing service

Offering an ironing service can be a brilliant way to make extra money, especially if you find ironing to be a relaxing task. Many people either don't have the time or simply don't enjoy ironing. That's where you come in, turning a household chore into a profitable venture. Whether it's work shirts, school uniforms or special-occasion outfits, people are willing to pay for that freshly ironed look without the hassle of doing it themselves.

Setting up an ironing service is relatively simple. All you need is a good-quality iron, an ironing board and some space in your home to get to work. It's also necessary to hold business insurance just in case you damage a client's piece of clothing. You can decide whether to offer a collection and delivery service or have clients drop off their laundry at your place. Plus, this side hustle is incredibly flexible, allowing you to iron when it suits you, making it perfect for fitting around other commitments, and your favourite show on Netflix.

Giftwrapping service

If you've got a flair for creativity and enjoy making things look beautiful, offering a gift-wrapping and nappy cake service could be the perfect side hustle for you. Gift-wrapping, especially around holiday seasons, can be a chore for many people. That's where your expertise comes in. You can transform ordinary boxes into works of art with your paper, ribbons and bows. But the creativity doesn't stop there. Nappy cakes are unique gifts for baby showers or new parents, made from layers of rolled-up nappies and adorned with baby essentials like bottles, bibs and toys.

The best part about this hustle is that the start-up costs are pretty low. You'll just need to invest in some basic materials to get started. You can work from home and use social media to showcase your creations and attract customers. Plus, you can offer themed or personalised options for an extra fee, allowing you to exercise your creative muscles even more.

Window cleaning

Window cleaning can be a rewarding small business if you're someone who enjoys working outdoors and doesn't mind a bit of physical effort. Believe it or not, sparkling windows make a big difference to the look of a home, shop or business, but many people lack either the time or the equipment to do it themselves. That's where you come in, offering a valuable service that brightens up buildings and puts a shine on your bank account.

Getting started doesn't require a massive investment. You'll need a few essentials like a squeegee, some cleaning solution and a ladder for those hard-to-reach spots. The great thing about window cleaning is that it's a regular job; once you've got a customer, they'll likely need your services every few weeks or months. And word-of-mouth can spread quickly, helping you build a solid client base before you know it.

WHAT ABOUT TAX?

If you already pay tax via your main job, do you also need to pay tax on your side hustles and second jobs?

At one point, while we had the Skint Dad blog as a self-employed business, Skint Mum was working full time, and had a part-time job cleaning for extra money. It may seem daunting having multiple income streams, but we promise, tax on a second job or if you're self-employed is not as complicated as it sounds.

Firstly, if you have a main job where you're employed and get a payslip (that's PAYE – Pay As You Earn), and then get a second job, you'll still need to pay tax on that extra income. The tax rate depends on how much you earn altogether and will be calculated by HMRC. If your total earnings push you into a higher tax bracket, you'll have to pay a bit more tax. Your second employer will take this tax out of your pay just like your first job does.

 Skint Tip: *It is not illegal to have two or even more jobs at the same time, and you usually don't need to notify your employer. However, some contracts may have a clause to prevent you from working for a direct competitor or supplier where it is seen as a conflict of interest. Check your contract or contact ACAS for free guidance if you are unsure.*

Now, let's say you're self-employed, perhaps you're a freelancer or have your own small business as a side hustle. You've got to tell the tax office (HMRC) about the extra money you're making. Unlike a PAYE job, the tax isn't automatically taken out of your earnings. You need to keep records of what you earn and what you spend on your business. You must register as self-employed on the gov.uk site and, every year, you'll fill out a tax return to work out how much tax you owe. You might also need to pay National Insurance, which is a contribution towards things like healthcare and your state pension.

There is some good news! If your self-employed side hustles earn you less than £1,000 a year you won't need to declare the earnings to HMRC or pay tax on it. This is known as the 'Trading Allowance'. This £1,000 cap doesn't relate to selling any of your personal items, it's purely for money you make on a business activity. Check the latest information on the gov.uk site or make an appointment with an accountant for advice.

In any case, the main thing is to keep good records and make sure you're putting some money aside to cover tax at the end of the year. If you end up earning less than £1,000 you've got some automatic savings. It's all part of being a responsible money-maker!

 Skint Tip: *Additional income may impact benefits you receive, including Universal Credit. You could still be better off overall, but you don't want any nasty surprises or to have to pay any owed money back, so be sure to declare any extra you make.*

8

MAKING YOUR
BANK ACCOUNT PAY

I t's not all about the side hustle. You don't always have
to be wheeling and dealing to pull in a little extra cash
here and there. There are a few other ways to top up your
monthly earnings. In Becoming Frugal we talked about
saving money by making lifestyle changes. Here we look
at how your savings can make you money instead!

There are loads of different sorts of bank accounts on
the market today and you can make free money from
the way you do your banking if you are smart about how
you do it.

SWITCHING

Gone are the days when you opened a bank account as a teenager and stayed with the same bank for the rest of your life. There are so many different types of bank accounts out there now, all vying for your custom, and many of them will offer you incentives to switch your account to them. Some offer plain cash if you switch, others give you gift vouchers or extras like travel insurance or mobile phone insurance.

Switching accounts can sound like a drag but most banks make it relatively easy for you to do and will make sure all your direct debits and other payments get moved over smoothly. The main thing to check is that the new account you're switching to still serves your needs.

Case Study

Skinter Gary has always wanted to make sure his money is working for him in the best way possible. He sussed out that he could make over £1,000 by switching bank accounts and taking advantage of the bonuses they paid when he did it. He started off switching one account but eventually switched to seven new accounts, all in the course of just a few months. Each time he switched he received a bonus as soon as he met the qualifying criteria. He has put his earnings from switching towards his dream of early retirement.

SKIMMING

Ever heard of financial skimming? In business, skimming money is literally stealing money off the top. But you can use the principle of skimming money from your own bank balance to create savings and earn interest, all without noticing you're doing it. It's a kind of savings side hustle and we love it because it takes the sting out of putting money aside.

With skimming, you round up your balance to the nearest whole number and transfer the odd amount into a savings account. For example, if you have £128.45 in your bank account, you could transfer £8.45 into your savings account. Or if things are a little tight, transfer just the odd 45p. Leave this money in your savings account for as long as possible; ideally, you'll just forget about it because it's such a small amount. The interest you'll earn on the amounts you deposit is an added bonus.

 Skint Tip: There are a number of apps such as Chip, Plum and Moneybox that do the skimming for you and invest your tiny amounts in stocks and shares ISAs or even put them into your

pension. A lot of bank accounts offer a round-up service now and put your skimmed cash into your savings account for you. As always, do your research and find the best deal for you.

GET A LISA (LIFETIME ISA)

One of the most generous sources of free money we know of out there is a £1,000 (yes, £1,000!) bonus you can get from the government every year (yes, every year!) if you open a savings account called a Lifetime ISA.

LISAs are aimed at people who are saving for a deposit on their first home or, if you are already a homeowner, you can use it to save for later life. You also need to be over eighteen and under thirty-nine years old, and you can't withdraw money from it unless it's for a house purchase or you're over sixty. But you can keep saving for thirty-two years, so if you meet the criteria and you are saving for your first place, a LISA could earn you up to £32,000 in free cash (assuming you save for thirty-two years and deposit the maximum of £4,000 a year). That is one serious side hustle!

To get the full £1,000 a year you'll need to deposit £4,000 into your LISA in a single tax year (April to April). But if you haven't got that much to put aside it doesn't matter, the government will still give you a 25 per cent bonus on anything you save, up to the £4,000 threshold.

OPEN A HELP TO SAVE ACCOUNT

A Help to Save account is a special type of savings account in the UK designed to help people on lower incomes save money. If you qualify, this account offers you an extra bonus from the government just for saving! How brilliant is that? For every £1 you put into the account, the government will give you a bonus of 50p. You can save up to £50 a month, and the bonuses are paid after two years and four years.

This account is really useful if you're receiving certain benefits like Universal Credit or Working Tax Credit. You can open a Help to Save account online and it's pretty straightforward to manage. But remember, you can only take the money out without losing the bonus after those two- or four-year periods.

So, it's like getting free money for being good at saving! If you're looking to build up a rainy-day fund or save for something special, a Help to Save account can give your savings a nice little boost.

FIND LOST MONEY IN OLD ACCOUNTS

Did you have a bank account as a child that you have forgotten all about? Did a distant relative once buy you Premium Bonds that you have no idea how to retrieve?

You are not alone. There are millions of pounds sitting in dormant, unclaimed and unchecked accounts across the UK.

Perhaps one of them has your name on it? If so, it's time to get reunited with your money!

If you don't touch an account for a long time (around fifteen years) the assets (your money) will usually get transferred to what's called a Dormant Asset Scheme. This scheme tries to reunite you with your cash. In 2022, the Dormant Assets Act expanded the scope of the Scheme to include assets from insurance and pensions, investment and wealth management, and securities – so it's not only your old bank accounts that could be sitting waiting for you.

Hunting out old accounts isn't always straightforward and you may need to mine the depths of your memory to pull up information! But start by contacting the firm that held your account, or use the My Lost Account website to track down old accounts.

 Skint Tip: *The more information you can supply about old addresses, account details, etc., the better. And if you got married and changed your name remember the account might be in your old name!*

Remember: banks are holding YOUR money and when you find it, they have to give it back.

FROM SKINT TO SELF-EMPLOYED

Being self-employed and in charge of your own destiny is often framed as the ultimate work–life aspiration. It's true that we Skints love our new life running the Skint Dad blog and wouldn't go back to our old jobs even if they paid us (which they would have to!). But it's not always as easy as it seems to make the leap, and while people tell you about all the positives, like being flexible and doing something you want to do, there are plenty of other financial considerations to make before you decide you want to give up your job. Here are a few to get you started:

- Not having a regular income can make your personal budgeting complicated. You'll need to be really disciplined and make sure you have enough in your account every month to pay the bills, even if you don't get paid every month! Bear in mind that regular outgoings like direct debits and standing orders might not be the best solution for you when paying bills.
- You don't get sick pay or holiday pay when you're self-employed. Again, you'll need the discipline of a monk to make sure you have some back-up funds for if/when surprises happen.
- There is plenty of support from HMRC for self-employed people but it's still quite complicated

stuff and hard to navigate if you're new to things like tax and National Insurance. A good accountant or bookkeeper will always be worth their weight in gold, but of course, you do need to pay them. Be honest with yourself about how well you can manage this aspect of your new role and don't feel bad if you need to get some help. Businesses employ specialists to handle their finances for a reason!

- You can't just clock off when the day is over. If something needs to be done you have to do it and you can find your personal time dwindles as a result. The flip side is you can give yourself the morning off the next day if you need a lie-in (unless you have kids!).

We Skints took a calculated approach when switching to self-employment. While Ricky was a stay-at-home dad and Naomi was working full time, we began to build the business on the side. This allowed us to test the waters without risking our main source of income.

While we would have loved to have made loads of money fast, we realised it wasn't a realistic goal, so we made sure to build things up, not rush (and then potentially make mistakes), and we took time to grow the business. By doing this, we could make sure it was something viable, sustainable in the long term, and not just a passing whim, a fad or a one-trick pony.

We didn't go it alone, and we think it would be hard if most people tried. We spoke to friends, family and people who were doing similar things and who had experience in self-employment. This gave us valuable insights into what we could expect and what pitfalls to avoid.

One of the smartest moves we made was to build up a financial cushion. We saved money to cover at least three months of living expenses for an emergency, which took a fair bit of time, but also took a lot of pressure off us when we finally did make the jump to us both working full time on the business. If something went wrong, we had money to fall back on while we tried to re-boost the business or went back to job hunting.

To make sure we could sustain two incomes, we created financial projections. We mapped out our expected income, factored in seasonal ups and downs, costs, and assessed how much we needed to earn to maintain our personal budget.

Before taking the plunge, we thought about what could go wrong. Running an online blog ... Imagine if the internet went down? By preparing for the worst, like what would happen if the business lost an income stream, it allowed us to be better equipped to handle challenges.

But it doesn't stop. Once we made the transition, we didn't rest on our laurels. We were driven to make the business a success, continually developing new ideas, learning from experiences, and adjusting strategies as needed. Even today, we are still doing the same.

9

FROM SIDE HUSTLE TO SERIOUS BUSINESS

When you're busy earning, it's sometimes hard to step back and look strategically at what you're doing with your side hustles and extra revenue streams. Just as we did the 1p Saving Challenge, to make saving money more fun and give ourselves a goal, we decided early on that we'd put some challenges in place to help grow the Skint Dad blog and its viability as a way of earning money.

We'd started to use Google Ad Sense on the blog and we were earning a few pennies here and there through advertising. We knew that using the blog as a platform for advertising was a great way of making passive income. We were writing the content anyway, and well-targeted advertising is never a bad thing for our readers. But we were still new to the blogosphere and we didn't have money behind us that we could afford to make mistakes with. So we decided to aim for something small and achievable: £1 a day in revenue from advertising.

Why only a pound? Well, for starters it's a whole number that we could easily visualise and felt like it was within our grasp. We knew we were working flat out already, but if we could make our content just a little bit better, write just a little bit more, and increase the number of views and click-throughs by just a few each day, we could reach our target of £1 a day.

This idea of tiny, incremental change is a well-known strategy in business and the world of sport.

Famously, in 2008 the British cycling team employed a man named David Brailsford to help take them to victory before the Beijing Olympics. Instead of making drastic, sweeping changes, Brailsford had the team implement small, almost unnoticeable upgrades to their existing way of doing things. He broke down everything he could think of that went into riding a bike and tried to improve it by 1 per cent. They got comfier bike seats, slept on better mattresses, and even repainted their bike truck to make it brighter and easier to keep clean. Without making any major changes to their training programme but improving in other small areas, the team went on to win twelve gold medals in Beijing and even more at the London Olympics four years later!

We're not Olympic sportspeople and chances are nor are you, but there is something in this story that we can all learn from. If you can achieve tiny, marginal gains – maybe just 1 per cent at a time – it will lead to a significant, cumulative effect. So if you're not a gold-medal-winning cyclist but have a side hustle selling old clothes, how can you put this into practice?

Try this:

1. Give your side hustle a financial endgame. Instead of just letting the money trickle in here and there, think about what you want from your side hustle. How much extra do you need from it? How much do you think it could realistically provide? What goals can you set yourself? Thinking more strategically about the money coming in from a side hustle, no matter how small, gives you a sense of direction and reward when you can make it happen. Even if it's a small amount – £5 or £10 a week – set that goal and work towards it. You'll feel more motivated to achieve and might be surprised by how easily it comes to you when you focus on making it happen!

2. Apply the same logic as David Brailsford did with the cycling team to whatever you're doing with your side hustle. Let's say you're selling old clothes online. Break the job down into parts: taking pictures, describing your item and uploading it,

then posting the item. Now look at these aspects of the job individually – what can you do to slightly improve your performance? Can you add a couple more pictures or style the clothes in a more eye-catching way to improve the amount of views you're getting? Can you add a few more lines in the description to inspire your potential buyers? Can you speed up your postage process so your buyer receives the item sooner? These are all easy-to-make changes that can have a profound effect on the service you provide and therefore the amount of money shoppers want to spend with you.

 Skint Tip: *When you start to hit your financial goals, try upping your targets. Once I knew we could make £1 a day from our ad revenue, I knew that we could make £10 and £20, and so on. Keep moving forward and up in small amounts and you'll be amazed by the results.*

THE IMPORTANCE OF COMMUNITY

From the moment Ricky's first blog went viral, the thing that has helped us through the hard times is having access to the amazing Skint Dad community. Sharing stories and ideas with other people who were going through the same thing was a lifeline for us and made it feel like what we were doing was a team effort.

Obviously, we hope if you're reading this that you are already a part of the Skint Dad community, but even if you're not, we want to stress just how important and integral to your success, sharing your money-making journey can be.

This doesn't mean you need to share every single win on social media or bare your finances for the world to see. But we know from experience just how motivating it is to have other people cheering you on. We also know that most people are really kind and want you to succeed. And, who knows, sharing what you're doing could give someone else the inspiration and motivation to start something new and change their lives too. We believe that the amount of ideas and information that gets shared on Skint Dad, all for free, is as valuable as any business studies course or MBA!

So our point here is you don't have to go it alone. Even if all you're doing is renting out your driveway, there are other people out there who have been doing it for a while who can tell you all the pitfalls and ways to boost your earnings. It might be as simple as sweeping the driveway more often or tipping off your customers about a local shortcut. Whatever it is, the advice and support of others in the same boat is always worth having.

Next up: Start being smarter about managing your money!

Part Three

MANAGE MONEY

Money isn't something we're taught much about at school, is it? It's odd when you think about it, because money is such an important part of human life, it's the currency we all live by, and yet we don't teach our kids what to do with their money or how to look after it! It might explain why, later on, we adults don't talk about it much either. If you're anything like us, you probably grew up believing that money was something you don't discuss in public. You don't tell people what your salary is or even how much you spend on a birthday present, because somewhere deep in your subconscious there's this crazy idea that you shouldn't tell people what you've spent money on or how much you've got in the bank. It's nuts!

What's more, in our lifetime and with the arrival of the internet and smartphones, the way we all manage our money has changed beyond recognition. There are now so many different ways to 'do' banking, endless different types of credit cards and loans, insurance for everything and anything. Wealthy people and the super-rich have financial advisers who help them to manage their money and navigate the complex world of finance. Yet ordinary people like us are sent off into the world without a clue and expected to get to retirement without any debts and a big pension pot. It's hardly a surprise that we don't always manage it.

In 2022, statistics released by the Bank of England showed that over a third of people in the UK (34 per cent) have no savings at all. The figure for the younger age group (eighteen to twenty-four) was 47 per cent. That means that almost half of young people will need to rely on credit or borrowing of some kind if they lose their jobs or need money in an emergency or even for something out of the ordinary. Without knowing the risks or understanding the different ways of borrowing, it's easy to see how people can so easily fall into debt. We know how it happens, only too well.

That's why we are here, to share everything we've learned on our financial journey to help you manage your money. Whether you have worrying debts and don't know how to start dealing with them, you're wondering how to make the most of your savings or you just want to know how you're going to pay for Christmas this year, we've got you covered. And, if like us you find all the jargon around money management confusing and strange, we explain what it all means, to help you understand some of the common terms and phrases you might come across on your journey to better finances.

Ready? Let's go!

Skint Tip: *As always, keeping your budget updated and close to hand will help you make informed decisions. The more you can refer back to your budget and work with it, the more control you'll have over your finances. And control means freedom.*

10

BANKING

Technically speaking, you don't have to have a bank account. You could keep all your money in cash under the mattress and you would be perfectly entitled to do so. But bank accounts are how most of us keep our money safe and access our funds when we need to buy or pay for something. Very few employers will pay their staff in cash these days, and increasingly retailers are asking for card payment over cash. Like it or not, the move towards a cashless society shows no sign of slowing down. In 2022, a report by the banking body UK Finance predicted just 6 per cent of payments would be made by cash within a decade. So it's generally a good idea to have a bank account (or a building society or credit union account – and we'll explain the difference in a sec).

But how do you know which bank to use and when should you switch accounts? There are literally thousands of different accounts out there now, many of them doing the same thing, but some are better than others. We can't tell you which one to go for but we can help you make informed choices.

ONLINE BANKS

Sometimes called neo-banking, online banks are one of the best and most important innovations in personal finance. Being able to access your money from your smartphone or computer just makes everything more straightforward and efficient for everyone. You can transfer money, pay bills and track your spending, all from your phone. And because they don't have to run costly high-street branches, the rates and fees are usually far better than the old-school banks, making these accounts a win-win for us here at Skint HQ. However, for some people, the lack of visible, high-street branches can be a barrier, especially if you still handle a lot of cash or if you want to pay in a cheque. Luckily, you'll usually find most neo-banks offer a paying-in service via the Post Office or other high-street banks.

 Skint Faves: *We use Monzo because it makes budgeting using different 'Pots' a breeze and has great customer service if we*

ever need to speak to someone. Plus, it's free! Other top-rated online banks that consistently get the thumbs-up from the Skint Dad community are Starling (for overall goodness), Chip (for best savings rates) and Wise (for easy overseas use).

BANK, BUILDING SOCIETY OR CREDIT UNION?

Banks and building societies perform the same basic functions, in that they simultaneously provide a place to keep your money (current accounts and savings accounts) and lend you money (overdrafts, loans, credit cards and mortgages). The main difference between them is the way they are structured; banks are privately owned companies, whereas building societies are cooperative enterprises owned by their customers or members. Historically people saw banks as the place to do your 'everyday' banking and building societies were where you kept your savings. These days the lines between them both are more blurred than ever and most banks and building societies have their own apps and websites for online banking. Credit unions are smaller than banks and focus more on helping the local community and people who use them, rather than making a huge profit. Many credit unions offer current accounts, places to save your money, give you loans and have other financial services, but do not offer as much as banks. The big difference is who owns credit unions – they are owned by the people who use them, like you and me. That means they often have lower fees and give better interest rates on savings because they're not trying to make loads of money for shareholders. However, each one will likely have one branch, with limited opening hours, which may be inconvenient for you. So we recommend you approach them all without any preconceived ideas and just try to go with the place that gives you the right set of services for you and your money.

SAVINGS ACCOUNTS

Banks aren't only there for when you want to spend money, they're usually the best place to keep your money if and when you're trying to save up for something. Why? For the simple reason that they usually pay a rate of interest on the money you hold in your savings account. So without doing anything, your money is increasing in value simply by being in a bank. This is the number-one reason why you should save in a bank (or building society) instead of a piggy bank or penny jar at home (although in our opinion, nothing beats the 1p Saving Challenge for a kickstart to your savings! See page 97.) We talked a bit about LISAs and Junior ISAs earlier in the book, and hopefully you're well on your way to having a Sinking Fund (see page 16) for emergencies, but where's best to save and what do all the different options actually mean?

ISAs vs Savings Accounts. What's the difference?

ISA stands for Individual Savings Account and its main feature is that it allows you to save money – up to around £20,000 – without paying tax on it. The reality is that very few normal people pay tax on their savings and so an ISA is really just a savings account by a different name. That said, there are different types of ISAs that work in slightly different ways and pay out varying rates of interest depending on which one you save with.

Cash ISA: A Cash ISA operates in much the same way as a conventional savings account. Depending on the specific Cash ISA that you opt for, you will be paid a variable or fixed rate of interest, and some accounts have restrictions on the number of withdrawals you can make.

Stocks and Shares ISA: A Stocks and Shares ISA operates like a virtual shopping basket that allows your investments to avoid capital gains tax. You don't earn interest from your bank or building society; instead, your gains are dictated by how well your investments perform. Typically Stocks and Shares ISAs outperform regular ISAs, but this is offset by the greater risk in investments, and your savings could go down as well as up.

LISAs (formerly Help to Buy ISAs): If you're looking to buy your first UK home and you're not over forty years old, a LISA is a MUST. The government will help you save for your first home by topping your savings up by 25 per cent. See page 144 for more information.

Junior ISA: A Junior ISA operates in much the same way as a standard Cash ISA, in that you are paid a rate of interest on your savings. But the money cannot be accessed until your child turns eighteen.

Innovative Finance ISA: These relatively new types of ISA let you invest money into what are called peer-to-peer loans, and in many ways these are more investments than savings accounts. You get a high rate of return but you're also taking a bigger risk because you could lose money. Not for the faint-hearted when it comes to saving, and if you can't afford to lose money we reckon you're better off going with a more traditional ISA.

What's a peer-to-peer loan?

Peer-to-peer loans are just like bank loans only they're usually on a smaller scale and between individuals. P2P firms and their websites help to connect people and businesses who want to lend or borrow money. You can lend your own money to another person or a small business and they will pay you back over an agreed period with interest. Taking out a peer-to-peer loan is a great way to get funding quickly and without having to go through tedious funding rounds or applications. If you're a lender it's also a great way to get a better return on your money because the interest rates on this kind of loan are typically higher than those from a bank.

The downside of P2P lending and borrowing is that the risk of default is higher. The person you're lending to might not be able to pay you back and currently this kind of lending is not covered by the FSCS (Financial Services Compensation Scheme).

Find out more about P2P lending online from the Money Advice Service and always use an established P2P site.

II

CREDIT CARDS

Credit cards can be a bit like tools in a toolbox: they're really useful for certain jobs, but they can also cause a mess if you don't know how to use them properly or have issues controlling how you spend money.

Let's talk about the good bits first. Credit cards can help you build a good credit history, which is important for stuff like getting a mortgage to buy a house or even getting a mobile phone contract. They can also be handy for emergencies or for spreading the cost of a big purchase over a few months. And they can give you more protection and act as a safety net. Under Section 75 of the Consumer Credit Act, if you buy something between £100 and £30,000, if the item becomes faulty or doesn't arrive, or an event gets cancelled, your credit card provider must offer a refund. The idea is that you should never get in debt for something you've not had or that doesn't work. This even applies if you pay a small deposit using your credit card.

Now, on to some jargon. When you hear 'APR', it means Annual Percentage Rate. This is how much extra you might have to pay back if you don't pay off your whole bill every month. Lower APR is usually better, and you can get a lower interest rate with a good credit history. The worse your history/score, the higher the interest you'll be charged. 'Credit limit' is the maximum amount you can spend on the card.

But be careful! If you don't pay off the full amount on your statement each month, the credit card company will charge you extra money (that's the APR kicking in). And if you only pay the minimum payment, it'll take ages to clear your debt and cost you a lot more.

There are a range of credit cards available, and each one can be useful depending on what you need it for:

Standard Credit Cards: These are the no-frills cards. You get a credit limit, and that's pretty much it. Good for everyday spending, as long as you pay it back on time.

Rewards Cards: These cards give you points, miles or even cashback when you spend money. It's like getting a little free bonus for shopping. But be careful; sometimes these cards have higher fees or interest rates.

Balance Transfer Cards: If you owe money on another credit card, you can move that debt to a balance transfer card (for a fee). These often have a lower interest rate for a certain period, making it easier to pay off your debt.

These days we treat our credit card like cash that we already have. And we spend only what we can afford to pay back in full each month to avoid those extra charges.

That doesn't mean we have always used them properly. At first, we used one to buy a fridge-freezer after the old one broke down. We couldn't afford to pay it off in one go, so paid in instalments. This was manageable. But, two months later, we had to get a washing machine. With no savings to fall back on, it went on the credit card – it seemed like free money and almost felt like it gave us some breathing room. However, the next month, it got worse when the credit card statement landed on the doormat. Those manageable payments obviously got higher as we spent more, and we struggled to keep on top of even the minimum payments. Don't be like we were! Think before you pop in your PIN or checkout online. Always have a plan for how you're going to pay it back and keep an eye on your spending to make sure you stay on track.

So, are credit cards a good idea or a bad one? Well, it depends on how you use them. They can be helpful if used wisely but can turn into a money pit if you're not careful.

Do you know your consumer credit rights?

If you make purchases with any kind of credit card or store card, a personal loan or hire purchase agreement, you should probably get yourself acquainted with the Consumer Credit Act. This is the law that applies to all purchases made using credit (sometimes also referred to as regulated debt). Why do you need to know about this? Well, as people tend to buy expensive and important items using credit – think domestic appliances, cars, technology, and so on – it means the stakes are higher if and when anything goes wrong. A good example: we recently bought a new laptop for our daughter to use at college; we want to know it's going to be reliable for her and that should anything go wrong, we can get a swift and full refund or exchange. Knowing our rights means we have peace of mind when making such a big purchase and means manufacturers and retailers have to keep their standards high, too. Here are some debts covered by the Consumer Credit Act:

- Credit cards
- Store cards
- Store finance
- Payday loans
- Personal loans
- Hire purchase
- Catalogues

 Skint Fact: *If you fall into arrears with any of your consumer credit debts, your creditor has to give you a default notice and time to bring your account up to date before they can take any further action to recover the debt. If you think you've been treated unfairly, you can complain via the Financial Ombudsman.*

CREDIT SCORE

Credit reports are like school reports, but for your money habits. They show how good you've been at paying back money you've borrowed or bills you owe. This is important because if you want to borrow money in the future, the lender will check your credit report to see if you're trust-worthy and can afford it.

Now, the good news is, you can take a peek at your credit report for free! In the UK, there are three main credit referencing agencies that keep these reports. You can access them free with:

- **Clearscore:** free access to data held by Equifax
- **Credit Karma:** shows you your history for free from TransUnion
- **MSE's Credit Club:** see your report from Experian

It's always a good idea to check your reports across all providers as they can hold different information on you, and you can get a full picture of your credit history. Credit card companies and lenders don't send information about your payment history to all of the credit referencing agencies, so you may see one and think everything is fine, but there may be an error or a flag for identity theft on the other.

You'll often see a credit score on your report, which is like a grade. While it's a quick way to see how you're doing, don't just focus on the score. It's really your credit history that matters most. This includes details like if you've missed any payments or have a lot of debt. Lenders look at this history to decide whether to lend you money or give you credit, so you need to make sure any information held about you, including your name and address, are correct.

Should you ignore the score? Not completely, as it gives you a general idea of your financial health. But your credit history provides a fuller picture and helps you see what areas you might need to work on.

Your credit score can go up and down like a yo-yo, depending on what you're doing with your money. If you pay your bills on time, your score is likely to go up. But if you miss payments, borrow a lot or have other financial hiccups, your score can take a nosedive.

Your score can change whenever there's new information. For example, if you take out a new loan, that shows up on your credit report and could affect your score. Or if you pay off a chunk of debt, that could give your score a boost. It can also go down for other reasons, such as applying for too many credit cards or loans in a short space of time, so be mindful of when you apply and try to leave at least six months between applications, even if you've been rejected. There are trivial reasons as well, such as not using your credit card at all or closing down an old account, but these drops usually correct themselves within a few months.

Checking your credit report is like checking your money's health. Make it a habit to look at yours (at least four times a year), so you can catch any mistakes or errors or spot things you need to improve. It doesn't get recorded if you want to check your credit report all the time – I was looking once a week at one point and there was no impact.

12

PENSIONS

You might be thinking pensions are for old people, why should I care? But it's never too early to start thinking about it. A pension is like a long-term savings jar that you and sometimes your employer put money into. When you're older and decide to stop working or work less, the jar opens and gives you money to live on.

There are a few different types of pensions:

- State Pension: This comes from the government. You pay into it through taxes, and you can get it when you reach a certain age.

- Workplace Pension: Your job might offer one. Usually, you pay a bit of your salary into it, and your employer adds some money too.

- Personal Pension: This is a pension you set up yourself. It's like a special savings account, just for your older self.

You should start saving into a pension as early as possible. The sooner you start, the more money you'll have when you're older to pay the bills, but more importantly to relax and have fun with. It's like planting a tree: the earlier you plant it, the more time it has to grow. There are also tax benefits. The money you put into some pensions isn't counted when the government figures out how much tax you owe. So, it can be a smart way to save.

One other thing to get in order is any lost pensions. If you've changed jobs or moved house, the chances are that you've left a pension behind and the provider has lost track of you. Thankfully, you can use the Pension Tracing Service to locate lost pensions, and they will tell you who you need to contact to get it back. At the end of the day, this is money you've earned, and every penny will help when you retire. You also have the option to combine multiple pensions into one pot to make it easier to manage. Consider talking to a financial adviser about what to do with any found pension money.

13

INSURANCE

Nothing quite beats insurance when it comes to annoying things nobody likes spending money on. Still, like it or not, insurance is part of everyone's finances, especially when it comes to the big things like our homes, cars and pets. But what you really need to insure and how to find the best policy can be hard to know and it's all too easy to find yourself over- or under-insured.

Whether you're looking to insure your shiny new mobile phone or bag yourself some travel insurance, a key point is that auto-renewing your insurance might be convenient but it will rarely – in fact, never – get you the best price. Use comparison sites and Direct Line (which doesn't appear on comparison sites) to find the best deals. We know it's time-consuming and you'd probably rather be doing anything else, but it will save you money that you can spend on something else!

 Skint Tip: *Don't forget to use cashback sites to buy your insurance. It's all money in your pocket.*

CAR INSURANCE

Car insurance is a legal requirement so it's not an option not to have it – if you're in a collision or even just parked in the wrong place, police can check on the spot if you've got it and if you haven't they can seize your car. Basically, it's just not worth trying to avoid paying it! But as with other major financial products, there are literally thousands of choices out there and finding the most cost-effective one for you can be a minefield.

Here are some key points to bear in mind:

- Shopping around is a necessary evil. Yes, we know it's boring but it is important to do it properly. Use a good comparison site like Comparethemarket.com or a specialist broker like Chill.com. Take the time to look at a wide variety of quotes and you'll quickly become au fait with what represents a good deal.
- If you can do it, paying annually instead of monthly can bring the cost down, as can adding a voluntary excess on top of the compulsory excess

(although of course if you need to make a claim you'll need to pay this!).

- Look at how you can lower your overall risk as a driver and car owner. Can you park somewhere safer, fit alarms or reduce your annual mileage? All of these things make you a better prospect to insurers, who don't tend to like paying out if they can help it.

 Skint Tip: *Adding a second driver to your policy who is low-risk can really help bring down the costs. We're talking your mum or dad here – not your teenage son!*

- Get a policy that's linked to a black box. These telematics devices monitor how safely you drive and inform your insurer – if you drive safely it should help to keep your premiums down. Originally aimed at younger drivers, who have a higher volume of collisions, they can also be useful if you've recently made a claim or had a driving conviction. Ask your insurer about black boxes. The only downside, of course, is that it exposes irresponsible driving!

- Consider value for money as well as pure cost. Some policies offer extras such as breakdown cover and personal injury protection, so if you want these things it might work out better value for you to buy a more expensive insurance policy.

HOME INSURANCE

Mortgage lenders require you to have home insurance in order to qualify for a mortgage, so this is another one you can't exactly skip over. Even if you're renting, your home is where you keep most of your really important and treasured stuff, so this is also one insurance that is genuinely well worth having. But finding a cheap policy isn't always straightforward. Here's a little look at what home insurance is all about.

What is it? Home insurance is a broad term for three different types of insurance.

1. **Buildings insurance** pays you compensation if something bad happens to the physical building that is your house or home. Fires, storm damage, collapsing walls and damp are all examples of the kinds of things that buildings insurance can help cover the costs of. If you're renting or if you own the leasehold to your property but not the freehold, you probably don't need buildings insurance – but always check.

2. **Contents insurance** covers the costs of items within the bones of the building. Electrical appliances, furniture, clothes, photos, that old chair that was your nan's – everything! The cover you need will depend on the value of what's in your

home and how much you reckon it would cost to replace it all. You might think you haven't got much but it all adds up, so try to be realistic and honest with yourself when considering the value of your possessions.

 Skint Tip: *Not all items are covered by contents insurance! Maybe you've got a top-of-the-range bike or you work from home and have a lot of specific equipment related to your work stashed in the spare room. It always pays to check with your insurer whether this kind of stuff is covered.*

3. **Combined buildings and contents:** This is a combination of both types of home insurance and the one most people go for as it's easier to deal with one insurer and often comes in cheaper than having two separate policies.

 Skint Tip: *If you're renting and don't own all the stuff in your home (say the cooker and fridge are the landlord's) you're still going to want to have some kind of cover in place.*

 Skint Tip 2: *If you're a student or a young person you might already have cover on your parents' policy – check with them! Also, try to avoid paying monthly unless it's interest free, otherwise you're saddling yourself with what is basically a loan.*

LIFE INSURANCE

Life insurance is basically a way of ensuring all your costs and debts (especially a mortgage – that's why they want you to have it!) are covered if you die and that any dependants are looked after. If you haven't got children or a big mortgage, you may not even need life insurance. It's probably better to put the monthly cost into savings or spend it on something else. But if you're a parent and worry about the kids having a home should the worst happen, it's a good idea.

As with other insurances, use comparison sites to get the best deal. The younger you can start the cheaper it will be – insurers prefer young people who are less likely to call on their policy than older folks!

OTHER INSURANCES

There is probably an insurance for everything – but you don't need to collect them like Beanie Babies! Insurance is a safety net against something going wrong, but what is the likelihood of that happening? Is the risk worth the expense? Would it be better to deposit the premiums you would pay into a savings account and use these to repair/replace or cover the costs of whatever it is?

Other insurances could include private health, dental,

pet, travel, income protection, critical illness, gadget cover, bike insurance, wedding insurance and more. You may consider that it's a worthwhile need for you, but be sure to read the fine print and make sure it's affordable.

14

WHEN THINGS GO WRONG

DEBT AND HOW TO HANDLE IT

In many ways, debt saved the Skint family. It was only when we got into so much debt – all £40,000 of it – that we finally knew we had to do something about it. Debt may be why you are reading this book. It's what started the Skint Dad blog and eventually propelled us to take control of our finances and our lives. Because of debt, our family has woken up to living. We now communicate better, we play with our kids instead of fobbing them off with gifts we can't afford. It has made us resilient and hungry to succeed in everything we do.

But debt is not a nice place to be, and we don't

recommend anyone follows the same path as us. We know just how debilitating and miserable it can feel to owe a lot of money with no clear way of paying it back. It affects every aspect of your life. We couldn't go to the supermarket without standing paralysed by fear at the checkout, wondering if there'd be enough money on our credit card to pay for the food. It got to a point where all we thought about was debt. Which credit card could we use to buy food this month? Could we get another payday loan to pay off the last payday loan? We were genuinely in a bad way and it seemed like there was no way out. A knock at the door and we both automatically assumed it was a debt collector when it was just the postman. We worried that a person parked in the car across the road was waiting for us to go outside to ask us for money back on a loan we had defaulted on. Even when we got paid, we worried that the money would get taken back by the bank to clear the overdraft we lived on, leaving us with no money to pay rent, get to work, eat.

There is a very real link between debt and poor mental health. In 2018 the NHS ran an Adult Psychiatric Morbidity Survey and found that people in problem debt are three times more likely to consider taking their own life. In that year alone 100,000 people had attempted suicide because of the debt they were in.

These shocking statistics show just how toxic and damaging problem debt can be. But it doesn't have to be like this. We know now that there is help out there and that debt doesn't need to be something that has such a terrible impact. We wouldn't ever wish to return to the kind of debt we were in, but it did teach us a thing or two about how to handle it and importantly, make our way out of it. We're going to share everything we know with you here.

 Skint Tip: *First, avoid getting into debt!* *It sounds obvious but prevention is better than cure. If you can avoid debt in the first place, you won't have to deal with it. It seems like there is some credit card or Buy Now Pay Later in a shop offering to lend you money everywhere you look these days and we understand how easy it can be to take out a payday loan to get you through.*

This is where all of the things we talked about in Parts One and Two come in handy. Before you take out that loan, have a think about what you can do instead to either cut down your outgoings or generate some extra money with a side hustle or a second income.

And practise saying no. It sounds easier than it is. We're a polite nation and we are all guilty of agreeing to do things we don't really want to do or can't actually afford.

Whether it's going out for dinner with friends or buying that magazine the kids want in the supermarket, saying yes often feels so much easier than saying no. But the knock-on effect (debt) is never as easy to deal with. Start flexing your 'no' muscle a bit more and see what happens.

If you struggle to say no to things, try taking a moment before you make that purchase or commit to that event. The scarcity impulse (page 29) can cause chaos for your bank balance when you're trying to make a sensible decision. Simply stepping away from the potential spending for a moment can give you the mental space you need to see more clearly. Often just a few minutes is all you need to realise you don't actually want to buy that dress or pay for that ticket to the thing you don't really want to see.

 Skint Fave: *Mr Skint is a big fan of the author Mark Manson. In his book* The Subtle Art of Not Giving a F**k *he suggests that when you're worrying over something you should ask yourself this question: 'Is this going to matter in ten years?' If it won't, then he says you probably shouldn't be worrying about it. Get over it and move on. I think you can apply the same thinking to spending money. Every time you find yourself about to shell out for something, ask yourself if what you're about to buy will be important to you in ten years. It doesn't even have to be ten years; it could be just a year or a week. The point is not the length of time but the longer-term significance of what you're spending your money on. Try it – it really makes you think!*

DEBT: THE WAY OUT

If, like the average UK household, you find yourself in debt, follow these steps to take back control of your finances and deal with the debt that is making your life a misery.

Get a grasp of your financial situation

We can't say it enough: knowing where you stand financially is so important. Not only will you be able to work out how much you can afford to pay back (and in what time period), you will also be able to spot problems before they arise. Keep working with your budget and get a really clear picture of what's coming in this month and what is going out.

Take responsibility

Yes, lenders can be irresponsible and make it too easy for ordinary people to get into debt. But ultimately it is your debt and your choices that brought you here. Accepting responsibility for that, instead of blaming the banks or other people, is curiously liberating. There's a calmness that comes with saying, 'Yep – it was me. Hands up. I did it,' and not trying to blame other people.

Share, ask for help and stop caring about what other people think

For many years we kept our spiralling debt problems behind closed doors and never spoke about it to anyone. It was only when we began to open up to people that things really started to improve.

I guess we thought that telling other people would make them look down on us. But how crazy is that? Maybe some people will look down on you, but the point is: who cares? They are the only ones who care! If you're like us, you only really care about what your family and the other people who matter in your life think of you. The rest of them aren't important!

It was only when I stopped caring about what others would think of me and instead was honest with Naomi and my family that I felt strong enough to turn things around. We reached out for support from StepChange Debt Charity to help us know what to do. They are amazing and are a total lifeline when you think you've hit rock bottom. Even that first phone call – admitting the debt, the amounts, how we'd buried our heads in the sand, and starting to create a plan – felt like a weight off our shoulders.

Please reach out to them too; even if you don't want to tell them your name you can ask questions anonymously. They are really nice, kind people who don't judge and offer free debt advice.

Case Study

Sarah-Louise became debt-free in March 2023. She'd spent five years struggling with money worries that she felt were holding her back from living her best life. Her fiancé is a dab hand at using spreadsheets and making graphs so together they began to analyse their money visually. They made graphs showing where they were overspending and how much debt they had paid off that month. Seeing it in this visual way really helped her to create a greener, healthier financial future. Sarah-Louise is now debt-free and says the ability to monitor her spending was what helped her get back on track.

 Skint Tip: *NEVER pay for debt advice.*

There's a page at the back with all the details for StepChange and other organisations that can help you.

Talk to your debtors

It is all too easy, when faced with a barrage of phone calls and letters from your creditors, to ignore them and hope they'll go away. This is what we did, for too long. It takes a lot of courage, not to mention a lot of time and waiting on the phone, to talk to your creditors and explain the situation. But we promise you that communication and honesty are the best way forward here. Regulated debt is subject to the Consumer Credit Act and lenders are legally obliged to behave responsibly and help you find a way to pay back your debts. Take the calls, open the letters. Stop running and you'll find you feel better for tackling the issue head-on.

What to say:

- Go through security to prove it's you. They may have an old address on file, which used to catch us out.
- Ask them to confirm the details of the debt and original creditor, plus any additional charges.
- Not sure if it's your debt? Can't remember taking it out? It's not on your credit report? Ask them to send you the proof.
- Be honest about your situation (e.g. low income, job loss, health issues, other debts).
- Go through your income and expenditure (your trusty budget).
- Ask for options of a payment plan.
- Ask if they can lower the amount or freeze any other charges.
- Only agree to realistic payments that fit your budget – do not over-promise as you'll stretch yourself too far.

During any phone calls, be sure to take notes of who you spoke to and what the next plan is, or when you need to follow up with them. Also, try to stay calm. The person on the end of the phone is just another human doing a job, and while I know debt worries can make you emotional, try to keep to facts and actions. And, if you're not sure, politely end the call before agreeing to anything and get in touch with a free debt charity.

TACKLE THE DEBTS AND OVERPAY IF YOU CAN

When you're struggling for money it's tempting to stick to the minimum repayments and try to put out the smallest fires first. The trouble is, when you're paying off a credit card, it will take you for ever and a day to clear the debt if you only ever make the minimum repayments.

We used to think that we were doing the right thing. We'd pay the minimum repayment and were happy with ourselves that we didn't default, giving ourselves a mini high-five for being so good. What didn't click was that we were paying so much more interest on a monthly basis than the minimum repayment. It's all too easy to keep coasting along like this and imagining you're doing the right thing because you're not defaulting.

Can you find any spare money from your budget using

the tips in Parts One and Two? Use that towards overpaying your debt.

 Skint Tip: *Instead of sticking to minimum payments, try to visualise your debt repayments as a row of physical items in a shop. If they're all the same, would you buy the most expensive one, or would you try to find the more affordable one? Thinking of your debt as a take-home product can really help to change how you approach it.*

Avalanche or Snowball Method

Should you put your overpayments towards the debt with the highest interest (Avalanche Method) or start with the smaller debts (Snowball Method)? They both have their pros and cons, and it's about choosing what you think would work best for your mindset:

Avalanche Method: highest interest first

Simply line up all your debts and see which APR percentage is higher, then go from there. When clear, move to the next one.

Paying off debts with higher interest rates first can save you more money in the long run because you'll pay less interest overall. When it's cleared, you won't have the stress of the higher payments; however, it can feel like a long time to clear the first debt.

Snowball Method: smallest amounts first

Line up your debts with the lowest pound figure owed and throw overpayments to that first. Then, 'snowball' the payment you were making on debt one, and make that as well as the minimum you were paying on debt two, and keep going.

Paying off smaller debts first gives you some quick wins and may keep you motivated. When one is cleared faster, there is one less payment to worry about. However, you will pay more interest over time.

If you need to see a quick result to stay motivated, pick Snowball. But, if you want to save as much money as possible and are happy to play the long game, pick Avalanche.

Set yourself some goals

Psychologists have proved that setting goals is a major factor in achieving any kind of success. It's common sense, really. How are you going to get somewhere if you don't plot your journey? So how can you use goal-setting to help you get out of debt? You need to set big goals and small goals, and you need to be specific.

Big goals: Your main big goal, of course, is to be debt-free. But this is too vague. It's all very well saying, 'I'm going to get out of debt,' but when you've got a lot of debt that can feel overwhelming and unachievable.

You'll give up and keep spiralling into more debt. Instead, try setting yourself a big goal that says something like: 'I'm going to cut my debt by 25 per cent within twelve months.' This is still a major goal, but it's also specific and, depending on the scale of your debt, more realistic and achievable.

Small goals: So you've got your big vision to slash your debt but you're probably also going to need to make some behavioural changes to get there. We talked in Part Two about making small, incremental changes to the way you do things when you're trying to make money (see page 151). This technique also applies to getting out of debt. Maybe it's about saying you're going to save an extra £10 a week by not buying coffee out, or maybe it's about saying you're going to check your account balance every day instead of ignoring it and burying your head in the sand. We can't tell you what your small goals should be, but they should support your overall big goal and be something you feel you can genuinely achieve within the context of your daily life.

Use cash wherever you can

It's getting harder and harder to use cash, but real money is your friend when debts start to mount. Why? Quite simply because you know where you are with it. With cash, you can clearly see how much money you have and this awareness leads to more care and control over your spending. Once your money is gone, there's no risk of accidentally dipping into an overdraft, or having to pay off purchases at the end of the month, as you do with a credit card.

The use of cash reminds you that the transaction you are making is real. This can prompt you to reevaluate purchases when you're physically handing over your hard-earned cash. This simple habit can change your perception of purchasing and provide you with greater clarity and control over your finances.

 Skint Tip: *Work out what you need for the week and draw out cash from the cashpoint. We know – old-school! See if you can spend less than you've got in your purse. You might even enjoy the challenge.*

Celebrate your wins

Paying off debts can be a real slog. There's always someone on social media bragging about how they cleared their debts in three weeks with some bogus side hustle. But take it from us, genuinely clearing your debts takes time and hard work. This is why it's so important to stop and look down the mountain from time to time, to see how far you've come. Acknowledging your efforts and celebrating (ideally with a free activity like a walk with a friend) will help you to keep going when it all seems like too much.

 Skint Tip: *What we found very important was to celebrate the wins. We cut back and stretched for so long, it felt like there was no end in sight, and it consumed our every moment. However, by setting a goal and then achieving it, it gave us a small victory. We'd celebrate by spending some money on a nice treat for the family such as a takeaway or a cinema trip – it felt like a luxury!*

 Skint Tip 2: *Debt is temporary. We play a game with the girls where we go through a tunnel on the train. As soon as we enter into it, we have to hold our breath and we can't let it out until we're back in daylight.*

Sometimes that's how debt makes you feel. It suffocates you, and it feels like you'll never make it into the light. But no tunnel goes on for ever. Everything changes. Keep clearing away that debt and soon you will find you can breathe and hold your head up high in the light again.

BANKRUPTCY

If your debts become overwhelming it can be tempting to consider declaring yourself bankrupt. But what is bankruptcy and is it always the get-out-of-jail-free card people think it is?

The answer, of course, is no. Going bankrupt is not a decision you should take lightly as it has serious implications and some negative long-term effects. It is important to understand the pros and cons of bankruptcy before making a decision.

Bankruptcy: what is it?

Bankruptcy is a legal process that allows someone in severe debt, that they are unable to repay, to restructure or eliminate their debt. It currently costs around £700 to become legally bankrupt. If you have debts of less than £30,000, a Debt Relief Order (which costs around £100) may be a better option. Always speak to a free debt counsellor before going down any of these routes without advice.

Going bankrupt has plenty of pros. It can mean a fresh start, and protection from creditors. Once you have filed for bankruptcy, creditors can't contact you or take any further legal action against you. You get lower interest rates on any future loans or credit you take out and in some cases your monthly bills can be reduced to a more manageable amount. Bankruptcy can also provide peace of mind by giving you a way to resolve your debt and get back on track financially.

But bankruptcy can also create difficulties. Your bank accounts can be frozen and your credit files can be affected for up to six years, or even longer if it's extended, making it difficult to get major credit like a mortgage. Worse, your assets can be seized and sold off to pay your debts. Your house can be repossessed and any other expensive items in your house can be taken in lieu of payment.

You may be required to attend mandatory credit counselling sessions and your ability to obtain employment may be affected as some employers won't hire people with bankruptcy on their record. And bankruptcy may not discharge all of your debts, such as student loans or child support payments.

What are the alternatives?

If the thought of losing your home and possessions doesn't exactly appeal, you might want to consider some alternatives to getting out of severe debt.

Debt Relief Order: This is a kind of soft-bankruptcy that can help to reduce your debts and stop creditors chasing you. It's especially good for people with smaller liabilities but it will stay on your credit file for six years. Talk to a debt counsellor like StepChange or Citizens Advice to see if this is the right solution for you.

Debt consolidation loan: A debt consolidation loan might be a great way to become more financially stable, but you will need a good credit history to access one.

Government help: If you are struggling with your monthly repayments for your debt, there is some help available from the government. Speak to your creditors about the Breathing Space (Debt Respite Scheme) to get protection while you come up with a debt plan.

If you are on a low income or benefits, you may be able to get help with your mortgage interest payments or council tax.

 Skint Tip: *There are LOTS of adverts online where firms promise to write off 80 per cent of your debts through a government scheme. They're advertising an Individual Voluntary Arrangement (IVA) and the company selling them makes a lot of money out of you. Around 30 per cent of IVAs fail, so it's definitely worth taking advice (and never paying).*

SHOPPING ADDICTIONS

Having an addiction to spending is a very real affliction that is affecting more and more of us. As with alcohol, drugs and gambling, shopping – by which we mean compulsively purchasing new things that you don't need and probably can't afford – can provide a brief moment of joy and relief from mental health conditions like anxiety and depression. But as with other addictions it can also have damaging long-term effects.

Because we all shop and because we are encouraged by banks and politicians to get out there and spend, it is something that can often hide in plain sight and creep up on you or a loved one, seemingly out of nowhere. Signs of someone struggling with a shopping addiction can be hard to spot but can include things like hiding purchases, throwing away correspondence from the bank, hoarding and seeming euphoric after making a purchase.

We always recommend you get professional help if you think your spending habits are out of control. We know exactly how easy it is to find yourself in this situation and how difficult it can be to get out of it – you need the skilled support of a professional to help you out here. But if you're at the stage where you're just a bit worried about your spending habits and want some advice on how to nip it in the bud, here are a few hard-won ideas of our own:

- Do no-spend days. As the name suggests these are days where you simply don't spend any money. It sounds so much easier than it is! But give it a go and see if you can get through twenty-four hours without spending anything. Obviously if you have direct debits or payments going out, you'll need to make sure they don't get affected, but apart from that see if you can spend absolutely zero for a whole day. This not only saves you money but it helps you get into the habit of walking away from purchases and opportunities to spend. It trains your 'no' muscle.

- Squirrel your money away. As soon as you get paid it can be tempting to skip down to the shops and splash out on a payday treat. Instead, ping that money into your savings account sharpish. Some people use the saying 'pay yourself first' and this is really handy when looking for the motivation here. Restricted-access savings accounts can also help if you want something that makes it difficult to get at your money!

- Leave your money at home. This sounds obvious but actually how often do you go out without your card or wallet? And if you've got Apple or Google Pay on your phone it's practically impossible not to have some way of paying on you. But give it a go. If you're going to work and you've got a packed lunch and your travel is all sorted out, what else do you need money on you for? Like a no-spend day, this helps you get into the mindset of being spend-free.

If you're worried about your spending see page 215 for useful contact details.

15

PLANNING FOR THE FUN STUFF

Just as you plan for your week at work, your holidays or your next big shop, it's important to incorporate an element of planning for the big moments into your financial life. Before we started Skint Dad, we didn't use to plan anything much to do with our money. We just kind of lurched from one bill to the next! But it turns out that putting your head in the sand and your fingers in your ears is not an effective way to make money go as far as possible!

You don't have to share your bank balance with everyone in the world and start a blog like we did, but you can begin to introduce some planning around some of the big things in life, so that when they happen you're ready and waiting with the money you need to cover them. We're talking Christmas, birthdays, weddings, summer holidays and yes, even funerals. Knowing you've got some money tucked away for these things, and that you have a plan in place to cover them, is a great feeling and we want you to have it.

SUMMER HOLIDAYS

We all deserve a holiday from time to time and in fact taking a break is an important part of a healthy lifestyle, so don't feel bad for needing and wanting a holiday. But if you're a parent, you know only too well that the word holiday often has very little to do with the six-week stretch of no-school that we all face every summer! Trying to organise work and childcare for this long is both time-consuming and extremely expensive. You don't have to spend fortunes to get through it but being able to go out for the day with the family or put the kids into activities so you can work requires some serious financial forethought. Whether you're planning a sunshine break or just hoping to get through the school holidays in one piece, here are some thoughts on saving for the summer:

1. Keep working your budget. This is where those months-in-advance pages in your budget start to earn their keep. Being able to look ahead and visualise what's happening for your finances in July and August is the first and most important step to being able to sail through the summer

months. If you haven't already set up your budget with twelve months' worth of plans then do it now! You won't regret this one.

2. Think ahead. Start a new 1p Saving Challenge at the start of the school holidays this year to save enough for next year. It's not an overnight reward but it's a great feeling to know you've got next year covered already.

3. Book any holidays as far in advance as you can and find out about paying in instalments. A lot of holiday operators let you pay in instalments if you book in advance. This is obviously a godsend if you want to have something to look forward to and you're prepared to lock it down early. The important thing is to include your monthly payment in your budget – you don't want to miss payments as your holiday can be at risk. And make sure your instalments are interest free, otherwise you'll end up paying more.

4. Find all that foreign currency! Have you got odd euros and other pieces of currency lying around the place? Take a minute to count it all and you might find you've got lunch out or at least an ice-cream's worth of money to take with you. This one's also handy for tolls and parking.

5. If you're self-employed, going on holiday can mean losing income as well as spending lots. Offset this as early as you can by saving up,

boosting your side hustles and cutting costs wherever you can. If you're paying for cover staff while you're away, make sure you factor this in as you don't want to be hit with an extra massive cost as soon as you get home. This is one of the many ways being self-employed requires you to be an expert juggler!

6. Set out a routine with the kids. Although they're off school, it can still be useful for children to have routine in their days and weeks. Everyone knows where they stand and it can really help reduce the number of questions (and arguments) over what to do and when. It can also help you keep your costs down! Build in plenty of time in your week for free activities like drawing and crafting, heading out to the park and meeting up with friends. They'll still be excited about the day ahead and you don't have to spend a penny!

CHRISTMAS

There's a long tradition of saving for Christmas in British culture. As young employees, Mr Skint worked where there was a savings scheme that would help everyone save for the costly month of December. Someone would come round with a book and you'd pay in your money and then they'd go and pay it into the bank. By the end of the year everyone had put a bit away and made a little bit extra in interest. For many years the Post Office ran a similar Christmas Savings Club for the public. Happy days!

With digital banking and the boom in credit these schemes have mostly fallen away, but that doesn't mean you can't still save for Christmas. And for us Skints, knowing we've got the costs covered and don't have to spend the next twelve months paying off our credit card is pretty much the best present of all.

- Work out what you need and set a savings target. Put it in your budget and set up a savings pot that you can easily transfer money to. You're all set to save for Christmas.
- Buy your crackers, cards, gift wrap and anything else you can think of in the January sales (which start on Boxing Day!). The savings are off the chart as everything gets slashed in price to get rid of it. No-brainer.
- Invent some new, free, Christmas traditions. Maybe it's something simple like taking your family dog for a walk or playing a game, or maybe it's making mince pies together or paper decorations for the tree. Whatever it is you come up with, Christmas is all about these rituals with family and friends and none of them needs to cost a bean. The more of them you can introduce to your family's Christmas the richer you'll feel.

- Start your own savings club at work or with friends. It won't earn you much interest these days and relies on a level of trust and consistency so we'd suggest you keep it small, but it can be quite motivating to share the saving process.

- Get in on a supermarket Christmas savings scheme. If you've got a Tesco Clubcard, an Iceland Bonus card or any kind of loyalty card with a major supermarket (and if not, why not?) you'll usually get some kind of bonus points to spend at Christmas. Make sure you use them!

- Some local toyshops offer Christmas schemes where you can pay in instalments for that brand-new bike or Lego set. Start paying early enough and you could shave a significant amount off your Christmas-present spending in December.

- Go second-hand. Children don't care whether something is brand new or not. As long as it comes in a box they can sit in they're happy! Plus you can often pick up toys and clothes that still have the packaging and labels on. It is crazy to buy new for young children, so embrace second-hand and enjoy saving your money instead.

- Keep an eye out for offers on your favourite foods and wines throughout the year. Wine and alcohol can be bought in advance, as can anything that goes in the freezer and products like pickles, mincemeat, mayonnaise. You don't have to rush out and buy it all on 23 December! Being prepared and getting things done ahead of time saves you money and helps you feel less stressed all round. Winner, winner, Christmas dinner!

Case Study

Mum-of-three Heather was worried about how she'd cope in the cost-of-living crisis so she introduced a four-gifts-only rule for her kids at Christmas. Heather decided that instead of overspending on things they don't need and buying things just for the sake of it, she would give each of her children four gifts. She based the rule on a simple strategy, rather like the wedding mantra of 'something old, something new, something borrowed, something blue'. For Heather's children at Christmas, the rule is they get something they want, something they need, something to wear, and something to read. The rule has helped her shop smarter and stopped her from getting into money troubles at Christmas. But it has also made her think about her children's presents to make sure each one they receive is something they really appreciate and value. Far from feeling hard done by, they all love that they get thoughtful gifts and that there is more money left in the pot for Christmas dinner!

Whatever aspect of your finances you're looking at, there are some key messages from us here at Skint HQ that apply to pretty much everything to do with managing your money.

1. Keep going back to your budget. Think of it as your map to financial freedom, or your own personal guidebook to your money. Tweak it, change it, update it. Just don't ever ignore it – that's when you get lost.

2. Talk to other people about money. Whether it's friends and family or people in the Skint community, a problem shared really is a problem halved. Let's normalise talking about money and start taking the shame out of being skint.

3. Shop around, do your research. You wouldn't go into a clothes shop and buy the first cardigan you see. You wouldn't walk into a car showroom and buy the first motor on the forecourt. Money is the same – you can make choices and get better products that work for you. Research, compare, take time to think it through.

4. Practise abstinence. Whether it's a no-spend day or leaving your cash at home for a few hours, learn to live your life in the moment, without the constant need to spend. Take it from us – that's when things get pretty cool!

Conclusion

Well, here we are at the end of our book! Hopefully, you've enjoyed reading it but more importantly, you've started to bring some new ideas and techniques into your personal finances. Whether it's writing everything down in your budget, starting a new side hustle or finally opening that ISA, we hope you're starting to see the difference – both to your bottom line and to your own sense of confidence around cash.

We've tried to pack all the really important stuff into this book but there's lots more information and tips on the Skint Dad blog. It can be especially helpful to check-in there around specific times when money can be an issue – whether it's picking up ideas for a purse-friendly Halloween or understanding all the jargon in the Chancellor's Spring Budget, there's always heaps of seasonal and timely advice and know-how on the blog.

And, of course, we hope you'll come and join the Skint

Dad community online. Join us at Facebook or Instagram, and you can connect with other Skints all over the world, sharing your money wisdom and worries with what we reckon is the friendliest bunch of people you'll ever meet. You can always reach out to me and Naomi directly as well. We love hearing from you and we're here for all your money questions. There's also a page of other useful organisations and contacts for you on page 215.

Remember, money doesn't have to be complicated or secretive or something for other people: we all use it and need it every day! So the more all of us can start to talk, share ideas and be honest about money, the better off we'll be. Good luck on your journey to financial freedom and we hope that one day you'll enjoy making every penny count as much as we do!

Naomi and Ricky

Acknowledgements

First things first, we owe a massive thank you to our families. You're our biggest fans and the first readers of a random blog we started one evening from the dining table. You've been the backbone of this journey, making sure we've had breakfast when things have gone wrong, helping us have somewhere safe to live, delivering a slow cooker (which changed our meal planning lives!), giving a constant listening ear when we're deep in thought about budgeting, planning our lives for the future and everything else in between.

To the Skint Dad Community, you lot are incredible. Your challenges and triumphs, questions and tips, and real-life stories, have helped fuel our passion for making finance simple for everyone. And, most importantly, you, the community, have kept us sane on our own continuing financial journey. Your support helped keep us accountable as we cleared our debt. You're the reason Skint Dad continues to exist, and I hope this book serves you well in your own money-making and saving adventures.

We want to give a big thank you to Charlie for helping us keep an eye on things in the communities and helping them run as smoothly as possible – it's not easy running everything as a husband and wife team, and you've given us the option to have down time every now and then, as well as sharing your own wisdom.

Huge thanks to Sarah and Jill who believed in us, guided us through the process, listened, and have made sure this book is both helpful and easy to understand. We would not be at this point without your support.

Stuart – I love you man x

Thank you to you and Laura for not only listening to our dreams, ambitions, and random rants, but for getting involved too. You keep us grounded and we'll be eternally grateful to you.

And finally, to you, the reader: thank you for picking up this book and taking actions and steps towards your better financial future. If we can make a change – you've got this!

Useful resources

Citizens Advice (citizensadvice.org.uk) – for general advice and especially on benefits and entitlements

StepChange Debt Charity (stepchange.org) – free advice and help with debt management and budgets

National Debtline (nationaldebtline.org) – offers free and impartial advice on debts

Gingerbread (gingerbread.org.uk) – specialist financial advice for single parents

Money Helper (moneyhelper.org.uk) – UK government-backed advice service